SAINTS OVERCOMING SCRUPULOSITY

EMBRACING TRUTHS ABOUT MENTAL ILLNESS AND THE RESTORED GOSPEL IN TREATING RELIGIOUS-ORIENTED OBSESSIVE-COMPULSIVE DISORDER

KYLE N. WEIR, PHD, LMFT

Copyright © 2021 by Kyle N. Weir, PhD, LMFT

Published by Finegold Creek Press, LLC

P.O. Box 1272

Washington, UT 84780

All rights reserved.

No part of this book may be reproduced in any form or by any electronic or mechanical means, including information storage and retrieval systems, without written permission from the author, except for the use of brief quotations in a book review.

The information in this book is for informational and educational purposes and is not intended to be a substitute for professional medical or therapeutic advice, diagnosis, or treatment.

❦ Created with Vellum

This book is dedicated to my wife, Allison –
Thank you for all your love and support in balancing all my endeavors.

CONTENTS

Saints Overcoming Scrupulosity	vii
Acknowledgments	ix
Preface - S.O.S.: An Integrative Model for Treating Scrupulosity	xi
Introduction – The Many Faces of Scrupulosity	xvii
1. To Whom Shall We Go? Thou Hast the Words of Eternal Life	1
2. Faith as a Principle of Action and Power in the Face of Uncertainty	14
3. Phase I: Foundational Truths and The Gospel of Growth	30
4. The Questions that Haunt the Scrupulous: Perfectionism, Sufficiency in Repentance through Covenant Relationships, and Judging	48
5. "God-Attachment" and Family of Origin Work	72
6. Mindful Self-Compassion and the Compassion of Christ	101
7. Phase II: Cognitive Behavioral Therapy Treatments for OCD and Scrupulosity	121
8. Exposure and Response Prevention and Scrupulosity	131
9. Phase III: Acceptance and Commitment Therapy (ACT)	144
10. What Every Bishop or President Ought to Know about Scrupulosity: Consulting with Priesthood Leaders	161
11. To the Scrupulous Saint	173
Appendix – Resources for Mindful Self-Compassion	177
About the Author	179
Notes	181

SAINTS OVERCOMING SCRUPULOSITY

Embracing Truths about Mental Illness and the Restored Gospel in Treating Religious-Oriented Obsessive-Compulsive Disorder

Kyle N. Weir, PhD, LMFT
California State University, Fresno

ACKNOWLEDGMENTS

This book has been an intellectually enlightening, spiritually inspiring, and emotionally rewarding to write. I could not have completed this work without the assistance of several key people to whom I owe much gratitude. First and foremost, I am grateful to the therapy clients I have treated who struggle day in and day out with this mental illness, scrupulosity. As we counseled together and sought healing changes in thoughts, behavior, and faith, I learned much from them. Their willingness to grant permission to include their experiences (with names and identifying information changed, or course) is a brave service to the many others like them who struggle with this illness.

    I am deeply grateful to my wife, Allison, and our children, who have sacrificed to allow me the time to counsel, teach, serve, and write in my roles as a marriage & family therapist, professor, and priesthood leader. Additionally, Allison has provided much editorial assistance as I bounced ideas of her in discussions and in reviewing drafts of this book. Also helpful to me in the editorial process was my former student and friend Timothy Childs, who was diligent in urging me to pursue this dream. I am grateful to him for his support. Additionally, I am grateful to the faculty in my department at Fresno

State and the colleagues at Roubicek & Thacker, Inc. who continually encouraged me in this new professional path for me in treating scrupulosity.

This work addresses members' issues and doctrines of the Church of Jesus Christ of Latter-day Saints, but I wish to make it clear that this is not an official publication of the Church of Jesus Christ of Latter-day Saints. The views presented in this book, as well as any errors, are solely the responsibility of the author.

Additionally, while therapeutic ideas and treatments are reviewed in a general sense, this should not be misconstrued as an alternative to seeking professional mental health treatment, nor as a guarantee or endorsement of any particular model of treatment. The information contained herein should point those struggling with mental health issues of OCD, scrupulosity, or other diagnoses to competent professional mental health providers and also to their appropriate ecclesiastical leaders in the Church to resolve spiritual concerns. This book provides valuable insights and anecdotal information about others' experiences with scrupulosity, but should not be viewed as medical or mental health advice in lieu of counsel by localized treatment providers. Readers are encouraged to seek help from professional medical and mental health providers in their area.

PREFACE - S.O.S.: AN INTEGRATIVE MODEL FOR TREATING SCRUPULOSITY

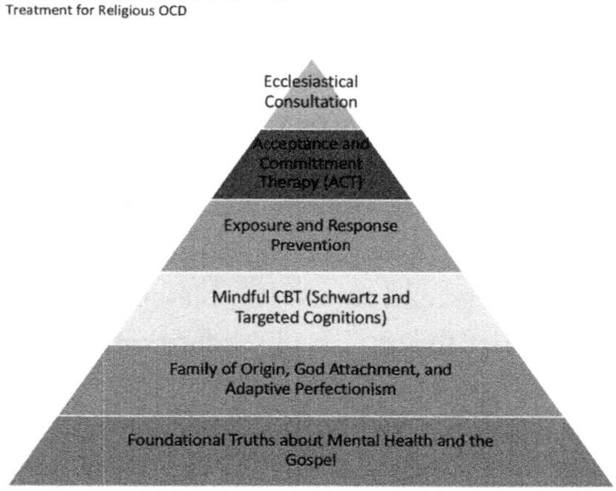

Figure 1 - The SOS Model for Treatment of Religious-Oriented OCD (Scrupulosity)

S.O.S – a familiar Morse code that has meant "save our souls" (and to sailors – "save our ship") over the ages. It is a spiritual plea oft repeated by the sufferers of a mental illness called scrupulosity – a subtype of obsessive-compulsive disorder (OCD) that is religiously oriented. Instead of compulsively washing hands, counting, re-checking, or keeping things symmetrical, this version of OCD is manifested in the form of intrusive religious obsessions and devoted acts of compulsive piety such as repetitive prayers or confessions. The sufferer of scrupulosity may plead in prayer or confess to an ecclesiastical leader begging that God will save their souls.

The problem they are experiencing – scrupulosity – is not a situation where their souls are in jeopardy. That's because their problem is a mental health issue – an anxiety disorder so unique that OCD has been given its own chapter in the *Diagnostic and Statistical Manual of Mental Disorders*, Fifth Edition (DSM-5) published by the American Psychiatric Association. The DSM-5 is used by psychiatrists, psychologists, social workers, marriage and family therapists, and counselors to diagnose and treat people with mental illness. But because the content of their concerns is religious in nature, it is easy for the sufferer of scrupulosity to confuse their mental health concern with their spiritual salvation.

This book suggests that for members of the Church of Jesus Christ of Latter-day Saints who suffer with scrupulosity, their "S.O.S." plea might better be converted to "Saints Overcoming Scrupulosity" rather than "Save Our Souls." Seeking help from competent mental health clinicians with the support of the Church member's priesthood leaders, these Latter-day Saints with scrupulosity can be helped to heal from this mental illness and enjoy the blessings and truths of the Restored Gospel free of the anxiety disorder that has often hampered or crippled them in their lives.

Let me be clear, scrupulosity is an anxiety disorder – not a spiritual or moral failing or weakness. It is a mental health concern that requires treatment, not a spiritual or religious condition that requires repentance, increased faith, or moral courage. The scrupulous often have an abundance of repentance, as well as faith and moral courage to the point of overflowing. But understanding and embracing truths about mental illness *and* Gospel doctrines restored to us in our day can bless the sufferer of scrupulosity to seek after and obtain competent mental health treatment that will aid in the alleviation of their mental suffering. The number of those who seek mental health treatment for scrupulosity is generally low compared to other mental illnesses.[1] If anything, they will likely turn to a priesthood leader first, not a therapist. They need to be carefully shepherded to a competent mental health provider who understands both their mental health condition and their religious faith, as well as be willing to ethically consult with the patient's ecclesiastical leaders. The scrupulous will often not trust a therapist who does not understand the complexities, nuances, and doctrines of their faith and can speak to those issues with the same authority they bring to mental health treatment.

Like all aspects of life, the Gospel truths provide a "Balm of Gilead" to aid suffering – even mental illnesses. Combining those truths with what research has shown about effective clinical treatment of OCD enhances the effectiveness of that treatment based on the previous experiences I have had as a marriage and family therapist working with the scrupulous sufferer and as an ecclesiastical leader in the church working with scrupulous saints in my ward. Understanding mental health treatments *and* Gospel truths can cause a cognitive paradigm shift to help the scrupulous better understand the nature of their mental illness and find relief. This book has the primary audiences of patients, practitioners, and priesthood leaders in the mind of the author with academic scholars as a secondary consideration. For that reason, the writing and citation does not follow traditional APA formatting, and the prose of the writing is more informal for readability.

Historically, one particular model of treatment – Exposure and Response Prevention or ERP – has been the gold standard of treatment for OCD. ERP has been shown to be effective in overcoming OCD from about 50-60%[2] of the time in one study by a leading expert of that approach to as high as 60-85%[3] of the time by another scholar. That is why any treatment model of scrupulosity should include ERP. The model suggested here in this book also espouses the use of ERP in the middle phases of treatment. Yet, other studies show that 25% of people suffering with OCD refuse to engage in ERP treatment, another 20% do not respond when receiving ERP, and yet again another 20% who do respond well during treatment relapse after treatment.[4] So, to increase the effectiveness of treatment outcomes, the *Saints Overcoming Scrupulosity* or SOS model of treatment integrates and encapsulates ERP with other effective treatment techniques – some unique to this approach and others tested by other therapists and researchers.

The SOS model of treating Latter-day Saints with scrupulosity begins with some foundational truths about mental illness and the Restored Gospel. In this Foundational Phase 1 the therapist and patient clarify the nature of OCD and its subtype of scrupulosity as a mental health concern, not a spiritual weakness. The therapist and patient then explore some of the cognitive misunderstandings LDS scrupulosity sufferers may have about God being a harsh, punitive, and overly-legalistic Deity that stem from views of Him that crept into Western Christianity through Augustine, Luther, and others (as opposed to Eastern Christianity's perspective on the Atonement of Christ being about healing rather than legalism). Based on what we know of God through the Restoration, those historical and erroneous notions about the nature of God are simply not true. The therapist and patient should discuss truths about their faith as revealed by Latter-day Saint prophets and apostles who clarify the comforting truths of the Gospel about the nature of God and how saints are to view our growth and progression in this life and the life to come. The therapist and patient explore the differences between adaptive and maladaptive forms of perfectionism and how to avoid the crippling effects of maladaptive perfectionism in battling scrupulosity. They work to understand the concept of judges and judgment, which means something very different in the way the Savior uses the term compared to the way the world views judgement. They then go into one's Family of Origin – the experiences in the family a person grows up in – and how that may affect something researchers call "God-Attachment" or the way people relate and connect with God based on attachment patterns with parents and siblings. The therapist and patient also look at stages of faith development by a researcher named Dr. James Fowler. Let me be clear that being religious does not cause OCD. Research[5] shows that people from a variety of faith traditions (and even non-religious people) can have scrupulosity. Yet, one researcher notes that even though "OCD is not more prevalent in religious populations, the presence of religious devotion can influence the focus and experience of obsessive-compulsive symptoms."[6] It is important to discuss with the patient that they would have likely developed OCD regardless of their faith development trajectory (given the nature of what researchers know about the biological and psychological origins of OCD). But Fowler's model shows that there is a healthy way to develop faith and an unhealthy form of faith development that influences whether a religious person sees God as harsh and legalistic vs. loving and full of grace. It is possible that harsh and punitive religious development may have affected their cognitive perceptions of God (as well as six key maladaptive beliefs that researchers suggest might fuel OCD), and may explain why their OCD subtype became scrupulosity rather than centered around handwashing, checking, counting, or other subtypes. The therapist and patient conclude the Foundational Phase 1 by implementing mindful self-compassion as the Savior exemplified as a means of preparing the sufferer of scrupulosity to begin Phase 2 and Phase 3 work.

In Phase 2, the patient and therapist begin working from a Cognitive-Behavioral paradigm. Strategically, the therapist explores some cognitive paradoxes that may benefit the patient. The patient is taught to utilize Dr. Jeffery Schwartz's Mindful CBT concepts from his book *Brain Lock*[7] including his four-step regimen. Once the patient has reached this stage of treatment, they are usually prepared to begin the "gold standard" treatment method of ERP. In this book, a separate chapter is devoted exclusively to ERP to highlight this effective form of treatment.

In Phase 3, the patient and therapist begin to work from a theoretical model called Acceptance and Commitment Therapy or ACT. ACT is an emerging practice that shows promise in the treatment of scrupulosity. Patients learn to "accept" that obsessive thoughts and impulses will likely continue in their life, but that they can follow a committed course of action based on their predetermined values that will avoid exacerbating their OCD through compulsions.

This book has a chapter about things priesthood leaders should know about scrupulosity (as they will likely be the first person the scrupulous saint turns to for help), as well as the "Ten Commandments for the Scrupulous" adapted to the unique circumstances, beliefs, practices, and views of Latter-day Saints. Finally, the concluding chapter appeals directly to the scrupulous saint with words of comfort and counsel urging them to seek help from competent mental health providers.

INTRODUCTION – THE MANY FACES OF SCRUPULOSITY

Aaron[1*] was an eighteen-year old young man preparing for a mission. He came to meet with me because the Missionary Department of the Church of Jesus Christ of Latter-day Saints wanted me to evaluate his mental health issue – Obsessive-Compulsive Disorder (OCD) – to see if he would be capable of serving a mission. After meeting with him, it was clear that he had a particular subtype of OCD called "scrupulosity" – a form of OCD where the obsessive thoughts and compulsive behaviors are centered around religious issues. Aaron needed more therapy sessions to get his scrupulosity to a manageable level. His biggest problem was that he wasn't sure if God was hearing his prayers, so he obsessed about praying "just right" following a formula taught to him since Primary. It also included his concern about praying with enough feeling and earnestness that God would hear and answer him giving him relief. He prayed over and over repetitively until he felt he finally got his prayers to be effective. This caused him to spend long, long times on his knees in prayer and often made him late for our therapy sessions. His scrupulosity generally interfered with normal functioning in his life. He also struggled because there was an attractive young woman at the store where he worked. She wasn't a member of the Church, but he found himself very attracted to her. He thought about her often and was afraid that his interest in her was sinful. When I asked about the nature of his thoughts toward her, it was clear he wasn't "mentally undressing her" or lusting after her. Rather, it seemed like the normal romantic attraction a young man would have for a young woman of the same age. It took a lot of work exploring both his spiritual concerns and his mental health problems, but after six months of therapy he was able to serve a mission in another part of the United States where he could receive needed medications and therapy while faithfully serving for two years.

Lisa[2*] was another person struggling with scrupulosity. Her parents called because she had dropped out of college due to her scrupulosity and was being treated in one of the best inpatient facilities in the country for OCD. The problem was that those facilities didn't seem to understand the unique LDS aspects of her religious obsessions and compulsions. In using the standard of care treatment approach (Exposure and Response Prevention), they showed her images of devils and other iconography more associated with other faiths to expose her to religious concerns, but the problem was that those issues didn't resonate with her and her issues. She needed someone who understood LDS theology, culture, and practice. Because she was from another state, we did a short-term "Intensive" (usually longer sessions of several hours over a few consecutive days or weeks) to address her uniquely LDS issues and then referred her to a therapist in her area for the follow up treatment. Her scrupulosity also involved repetitive praying and fears about the law of chastity. But in her case, she would start obsessing if she saw someone kissing on TV or in a movie (even in animated cartoons for young children). If she was in public, she would feel the need to go pray in a restroom. This made going in public difficult because she would often spend long periods of time praying in the bathroom while others waited for her, causing her to feel guilty and repeat the cycle of repetitive prayer all over again.

Another situation involved an older man who came to me to confess when I was his bishop. He told me he thought he had confessed everything to previous bishops, but then he would remember some small, miniscule detail and want to confess that sin all over again. Sometimes he would tell me he couldn't remember if something happened a certain way or not (and I often doubted if it happened at all as his memory was clouded in his old age and due to his mental illness), but he felt he should confess anyway. After several times of him coming to confess, I felt the Holy Ghost impress upon me that everything he had ever done prior to his meeting with me was completely forgiven and that I should tell him so. There was no need for him to search his past for sins. He had been forgiven (even though the few things I knew to be true that he did were grievous sins that he had long ago repented of). Not long after our last interview, he moved from my ward and then passed away. I believe that he did find a measure of comfort in my words, but I also recognize his battle with scrupulosity wasn't over after he left my office.

These are just a few of the many examples I've seen in my career and Church service of people suffering with scrupulosity. Throughout this book, I will try to illustrate how scrupulosity comes in many types and forms – what I call "The Many Faces of Scrupulosity." Some involve repetitive religious rituals like praying or confessing. Others might ruminate about whether or not something they did (or didn't do) was a sin or whether or not it is a "big enough sin" that needs confessing to a bishop. Still others might have an intrusive thought that they may have done something egregious in their past (even though they did not actually do it), but then begin to build "false memories" around having done the sin because their mind obsesses about it over and over till it "fills in the gaps" and gets them to believe they've done something they didn't actually do. Some may bump into a stranger on the street and then hours later obsess about how they can make restitution to a stranger they can never find for "injuring" them. They feel they will be eternally damned because they won't be able to fulfill that one step of repentance. Others may have intrusive, blasphemous thoughts that they can't seem to get to go away. There are so many ways that scrupulosity can present itself, but they all seem to involve a fear of failing to meet God's requirements or that they are not worthy of His love and salvation.

TO WHOM SHALL WE GO? THOU HAST THE WORDS OF ETERNAL LIFE

The suffering scrupulous individual and their family members often do not know where to turn for help. In the Latter-day Saint tradition, they have most likely turned to their bishop or other ecclesiastical leader for help. I often feel a tender compassion for our good bishops of the Church – they are the first line of defense for so many of the burdens the Saints struggle with. To make it even more difficult (and sweetly inspiring), bishops generally get no formal training in counseling procedures or techniques. They come from all walks of life – accountants, doctors, teachers, plumbers, and other productive and interesting professions that have little to nothing to do with pastoral counseling. True, there is the occasional therapist called to be bishop (like I was), but even that doesn't fully prepare a man for the expansive form of pastoral counseling bishops do above and beyond what normally occurs in a therapy context. No, the bishops of the Church are my heroes in part because they begin their service humbly unqualified for the position they are called to, must learn to rely upon the Lord for inspiration, and then grow under the tutelage of God the same way we all do in all the callings of the Church. In the words of President Thomas S. Monson, "Whom the Lord calls, the Lord qualifies."[1] But as inspiring as these bishops are, the situation of an LDS person suffering with scrupulosity is a complex phenomenon that not even the most experienced priesthood leader has had much familiarity with. For that reason, this book includes a chapter for priesthood leaders to help them know where to turn for assistance.

For the scrupulous saint, help must include their bishop or other appropriate priesthood leader because they hold the keys of a judge in Israel to help people know exactly whether or not a behavior or thought is a sin and how to repent, if needed. They are also there to guide and direct their members' spiritual patterns and practices of worship and Gospel living. They hold the priesthood keys and no therapist or other clinician can take their place. But on the other hand, the person struggling with scrupulosity has a mental health disorder (not a spiritual weakness or sin) and needs competent mental health treatment for that disorder, treatment that includes many things outside of the spiritual scope of a bishop's pastoral care. In most cases, it is not a spiritual concern so much as it is a mental health one, and so the resulting response might be better guided in a therapist's office than a bishop's office. To whom should the suffering scrupulous person go? The answer is simply: both. It takes a team approach to treat and heal from scrupulosity. Ecclesiastical leaders and mental health professionals must work hand in hand as a team to help the sufferer of scrupulosity overcome this malady.[2]

What Exactly is Scrupulosity?

In an academic journal article I once wrote with a research team of my students at Fresno State, we published the following definition of scrupulosity based on a thorough review of the minimal, but growing, body of literature on the subject:

> "Scrupulosity is emerging as a recognized subtype of Obsessive-Compulsive Disorder (OCD) pertaining to religious-oriented obsessions and compulsions. Essentially, scrupulosity is a form of obsessive-compulsive disorder, which manifests as religious

symptoms. Both scrupulosity and obsessive-compulsive disorder have two features that must be present in order to make an accurate diagnosis: (1) intrusive thoughts (obsessions) and (2) actions to neutralize the intrusive thoughts (compulsions). While many individuals suffering with OCD may experience a wide range of symptoms or issues, such as contamination obsessions, pathologic doubt, need for symmetry, sexual obsessions, and compulsive hand-washing/cleaning among others, people who struggle with scrupulosity primarily manifest their symptoms through religious-based issues (though they may exhibit other OCD symptoms, as well). Often scrupulosity is described as 'the doubting disease' or 'seeing sin where there is none.' The symptoms of this disorder are invasive and distressing in the individual's daily functioning and can impair occupational, social, and family relationships."[3]

Another set of researchers in this field more succinctly defined the disorder as: "Scrupulosity involves obsessive religious doubts and fears, unwanted blasphemous thoughts and images, as well as compulsive religious rituals, reassurance seeking, and avoidance."[4]

Though many people of faith may feel a drive for perfectionism, have anxiety about spiritual matters, or want to be careful about doing the right things in their life, this doesn't necessarily mean they have scrupulosity. Scrupulosity is defined by the deeply uncontrolled obsessions or thoughts that one cannot seem to remove from their mind even though they know the thoughts are very likely irrational ones. Pointing out the irrationality of their obsessive thoughts doesn't make the thoughts miraculously go away (in fact it usually simply exacerbates their pain because the sufferer knows the thoughts are illogical, as well, but they still can't make them stop or go away). Then the person with scrupulosity develops compulsive behaviors such as repeated prayers, overly confessing minute faults, or other religious rituals or practices to try to make the obsessive thoughts and fears go away, at least temporarily. Akin to the addict who can temporarily numb out the negative feeling with a drink, a drug, porn, or the next compulsive shopping spree, the scrupulous individual uses religious behavior to temporarily assuage the guilt or shame from some obsession they cannot control. They experience the relief of the negative emotion or thought going away and attribute the relief from their religiously-oriented compulsion. They keep reinforcing the compulsive behavior even if it doesn't make logical sense simply because the relief from the obsession is so temporarily rewarding. Unlike the addict, their obsessive-compulsive behavior such as prayer or confession is fully sanctioned and supported by the tenets of the faith. So, they feel confused and wonder how they can keep their faith, continue to follow God's commandments, be a "temple-recommend carrying" Latter-day Saint, and stop these compulsive religious practices without putting their salvation and Church standing at risk. But at the same time, they logically know that their "zealous" religious behaviors are harming their ability to function in life, on the job, at home, with their family members, in their friendships, and even in the Church. "Save our soul?" they plea, but their sanity, not their soul, is in jeopardy. What are they to do? The answer lies in first understanding the mental health issues related to Obsessive-Compulsive Disorder (OCD) and its subtype scrupulosity, counseling with their priesthood leader, and then seeking competent mental health treatment from a counselor or therapist who has studied and trained to treat OCD *and* who can talk with the sufferer about spiritual matters in a way that helps convince them scrupulosity is a mental health problem, not a spiritual one. This is the needed course of action for saints seeking to overcome scrupulosity.

OBSESSIVE COMPULSIVE DISORDER

Obsessive-Compulsive Disorder (OCD) is an anxiety disorder recognized by the *Diagnostic and Statistical Manual of Mental Disorders*, Fifth Edition (DSM-5) published by the American Psychiatric Association. It is *the* book all psychiatrists, psychologists, social workers, marriage & family therapists, and professional counselors turn to in order to assess, diagnose, and create treatment plans for our work with the mentally ill. While the formal list of criteria for OCD in the

DSM-5 criteria is expansive, the key critical criteria include the following:

"A. Presence of obsessions, compulsions, or both:
Obsessions are defined by (1) and (2):

1. Recurrent and persistent thoughts, urges, or images that are experienced, at some time during the disturbance, as intrusive and unwanted, and that in most individuals cause marked anxiety or distress.
2. The individual attempts to ignore or suppress such thoughts, urges, or images, or to neutralize them with some other thought or action (i.e. by performing a compulsion).

Compulsions are defined by (1) and (2):

1. Repetitive behaviors (e.g., hand washing, ordering, checking) or mental acts (e.g., praying, counting, repeating words silently) that the individual feels driven to perform in response to an obsession or according to rules that must be applied rigidly.
2. The behaviors or mental acts are aimed at preventing or reducing anxiety or distress, or preventing some dreaded event or situation; however, these behaviors or mental acts are not connected in a realistic way with what they are designed to neutralize or prevent, or are clearly excessive...

B. The obsessions or compulsions are time-consuming (e.g., take more than 1 hour per day) or cause clinically significant distress or impairment in social, occupational, or other important areas of functioning.

C. The obsessive-compulsive symptoms are not attributable to the physiological effects of a substance (e.g., a drug of abuse, a medication) or other medical condition.

D. The disturbance is not better explained by the symptoms of another mental disorder...".[5]

OBSESSIVE-COMPULSIVE DISORDER IS BASED in biology with other potential contributive factors. There are many competing theories for exactly which brain mechanisms cause OCD depending on whether the structure of the brain is examined or the activity levels of the brain are examined, but it is clear that neurobiological causes are crucial factors in the emergence of OCD (along with genetic and environmental factors – more of this will be examined in chapter seven).

At any given time, approximately 1.2% of the U.S. population will experience an OCD type symptom (internationally it ranges from 1.1-1.8% of the population).[6]

Prevalence rates that someone will experience OCD *over their lifetime* are higher and range from approximately 2.3% to 3%.[7]

Just looking at those individuals who suffer with OCD and scrupulosity does not tell the whole story. They do not live in a vacuum. Those suffering with OCD and scrupulosity have families – parents, spouses, siblings, children, and extended family. They also have friends, co-workers, and others to whom they are important. It is critical to understand that OCD and scrupulosity affects not just the bearers of the disorder, but also hurts those close to them. In my own practice, I've received phone calls, emails, and other communications from parents, in-laws, and other relatives about someone they love who suffers with scrupulosity. They are pained by the pain of their loved ones with the disorder. So, as we consider our baptismal covenant to "mourn with those that mourn; yea, and comfort those that stand in need of comfort..." (Mosiah 18:9), we must begin to view the wider, systemic effects scrupulosity has beyond the individual sufferer to their families, friends, and other meaningful relationships in their lives. In essence, scrupulosity is like a drop hitting the center of a still pond that reverberates ripple effects throughout society. Without treatment, the ripples seem to continue endlessly consuming their loved ones and friends into their grief and suffering.

. . .

Presentations of Scrupulosity

As a subtype of OCD, scrupulosity can appear in a wide variety of forms – what Abramowitz and Jacoby (2014) call the "Presentations of Scrupulosity":

"As with other presentations of OCD, scrupulosity is highly idiosyncratic and heterogeneous. Whereas one patient might turn to religious icons as a way of relieving obsessional fear, another might avoid such icons because they trigger unwanted blasphemous thoughts. Clinical observations suggest at least four (sometimes overlapping and not mutually exclusive) presentations of this problem:

(a) Generally ego dystonic intrusive thoughts (e.g. sex, violence, immoral acts, etc.) that are interpreted at least in part within a religious framework. The content of such thoughts might not be specifically religious, but the appraisals of the thoughts and associated ritualistic and neutralizing behaviors usually involve religious themes. For example, a man evaluated in our clinic experienced unwanted obsessional thoughts about engaging in sexual behavior with his sister. He appraised these thoughts as "abominations" and "sent by the Devil", and he engaged in repeated prayer when they occurred.

(b) Ego dystonic thoughts specific to religion… that would be generally considered blasphemous, and rituals and neutralizing strategies that may or may not involve religious themes. For example, an Orthodox Jewish woman we evaluated experienced distressing obsessional images of desecrating the Torah scrolls in her synagogue. To relieve her obsessional guilt, she avoided the synagogue, but engaged in compulsive hand washing rituals, as well as checking (calling the synagogue) and seeking reassurance (from the rabbi) that she, in fact, had not acted on her obsessions by mistake.

(c) Ego syntonic thoughts of a religious nature, perhaps concerning questions of faith or interpretations of texts, which develop into obsessions; and checking and reassurance-seeking rituals. For example, a Roman Catholic man found himself considering that abortion could be justified in some instances (which is contrary to the Church's stance). This led him to question his own faith and compulsively seek reassurance from his Priest that he was still a good Catholic.

(d) Obsessional doubts about whether religious rules and commandments have been followed correctly, or whether one is 'faithful enough'. The person desires to act in accordance with his or her religion, but fears he or she is not."[8]

IN MY CLINICAL work with Latter-day Saints struggling with scrupulosity, common examples include: repetitive prayer because the person is worried they didn't pray "just right" or with enough feeling; over-confessing sins (either confessing things that are not sins or fearing they left out some miniscule, irrelevant detail in a prior confession so they go in and confess repeatedly); checking to see if a behavior is a sin or not (or is a sin significant enough that it needs to be confessed to the bishop vs. just praying about it and repenting on their own); having intrusive blasphemous, violent, or sexual thoughts they cannot seem to rid themselves of and seeking to use compulsive religious rituals (e.g. prayer, singing a hymn, etc.) to neutralize the thought; having concerns about not being able to make restitution or amends in situations that make restitution difficult or impossible; being "over-zealous" about Sabbath Day observances with lists of "do's and don'ts" that they (and their family members) must strictly adhere to or feel damned; and being obsessive about fulfilling spiritual goals like "100% home teaching" (recently called "ministering") or going to the temple on a timeframe quota and then feeling overly-burdensome guilt if they failed in some slight area of these spiritual goals, among others.

While I believe in obeying the commandments of God with "exactness" (see Alma 57:21), people suffering with scrupulosity are like the Pharisaical Jews who looked "beyond the mark" (Jacob 4:14). The main difference is that the Pharisees compulsively obeyed overly-rigid religious rules out of hypocritical pride and self-righteousness, but the scrupulous sufferer does so out of insecurities and fears that stem from a mental health disorder that compels them to rigidly obey. The Savior's reprimand was replete many times over in the scriptures for the Pharisees and their prideful and arrogant self-righteousness, but the sufferer of scrupulosity merits His compassion and mercy. Too often the scrupulous focus on the Savior's rebukes toward the Pharisees and fail to see the difference in their mental health situation from the context of the unrighteous religious leaders in Jerusalem of Christ's day. So, helping the sufferer of scrupulosity to understand the context, intent, and meaning of those reprimands from the Lord helps the sufferer to stop misapplying those stringent rebukes to themselves, who are in a completely different context.

TYPICAL TREATMENTS for Scrupulosity

The most common form of treatment for scrupulosity is a type of Cognitive Behavioral Therapy (CBT) called Exposure and Response Prevention Therapy (ERP – sometimes called Ex/RP in the literature). ERP essentially involves a qualified therapist or counselor exposing the patient to the things that frighten or trigger them and then having the patient not respond with their normal compulsion or ritual. The patient agrees in advance to not respond in their normal way to the exposure of the fears and obsessions. While the exposure is being presented, the patient's sympathetic nervous system causes the heightened arousal, but after an hour or so of exposure to the fearful thought or other stimuli, the parasympathetic nervous system will eventually act to calm the patient down. As the patient experiences the calming effects without having engaged in their compulsive ritual, they begin to experience the fear diminishing. Over repeated exposures without compulsive ritual responses, the patient will become habituated to the exposures and the felt need for compulsions will diminish. While there can be some difficulties if not done well (for example, if the exposures are peripheral to the central or core fears, if the exposures are aimed at lower ranges of the patient's hierarchies, or if the therapist or others provide reassurances), in general ERP is seen as one of the most effective treatments for OCD with multiple studies supporting its efficacy. One of the leading researchers in treatment for OCD, Dr. Jonathan S. Abramowitz, Professor of Psychology at the University of North Carolina at Chapel Hill, indicates that success rates for ERP treatment range from 50-60%.[9] Greater detail about ERP treatment will be given in chapter eight.

Another emerging treatment approach with moderate success is Acceptance and Commitment Therapy (ACT). ACT (pronounced as one word – act – not A.C.T. because the subscribers to this theory like to emphasize "taking action" on the part of the client or patient in this approach) has been used in various ways to help people with OCD accept that their feelings, thoughts, urges, and obsessions will come and go, but that the person struggling with OCD can choose how to respond to those obsessions. They help the patient become mindful and aware of the feelings, thoughts, and urges, but to choose to take actions based on predetermined values and commitments that they have set that differ from their compulsions. They posit that while one cannot necessarily control the thoughts and feelings that comprise obsessions (and therefore must accept that they will come and go in their life like the waves of the sea ebb and flow), they can control how they choose to behave in response to obsessions and not engage in compulsions. They can instead choose to take "committed action" according to their predetermined values. One recent study found that treatment with ACT was clinically helpful in 46-66% of the sample after 8 one-hour treatments at the 3-month follow-up mark post treatment.[10] Again, further detail about this and other treatment options will be given in chapter nine.

Occasionally, if CBT, ERP, and ACT are not effective, some sufferers seek out other treatments like Dialectical Behavior Therapy (DBT), Eye Movement Desensitization and Reprocessing (EMDR), and more. These treatment options tend to be second line approaches when the first line treatments (ERP and ACT) haven't worked or if there are additional complex issues (like trauma) in addition to OCD.

While all of these treatments (and more) are important steps in recovery for the sufferer of scrupulosity, I believe they sometimes fail in treating scrupulosity among Latter-day Saints because proponents of these models are reticent to engage in preliminary steps to help the scrupulous cognitively reframe religious truths the scrupulous saint is struggling with. Some scrupulous saints may view God as a harsh and legalistically punitive God, rather than a loving Heavenly Father that supports and encourages their growth a development through the trials and errors of life. There are truths in the Restored Gospel of Jesus Christ that can aid and help the scrupulous saint to prepare them for better success with the ERP and ACT treatments that will ultimately ameliorate their mental health concerns. Also, exploring the concepts of adaptive and maladaptive perfectionism, judgement, family of origin issues and "God-attachment," and self-compassion enable the sufferer to cognitively restructure and understand their mental health issues in a new, uplifting light. By embracing truths about mental illness and the Gospel (what I call Phase I), the scrupulous saint can be better prepared for Mindful CBT, ERP, and ACT work in Phases II and III.

Now let me be clear, I am not suggesting that saying more effective prayers or getting a priesthood blessing is the end-all-be-all cure for scrupulosity. Rather, what I am suggesting is that there are some preliminary spiritual and doctrinal reframes and understandings that must be laid as a *foundation* for the subsequent successful treatment of scrupulosity through methods like Mindful CBT, ERP, ACT, DBT, and others. I am arguing that it is necessary to first "meet the client or patient where they are at." As a therapist, I must first join or connect with them and build a relationship of trust (what therapists often call a "therapeutic alliance") by being willing to hear their spiritual concerns, address any misconceptions they have, teach pure doctrines that embrace a healthy perspective on faith rather than a fearful and rigid religiosity, and address any attachment concerns (including what therapists are beginning to explore in a concept called "God-attachment") in order to prepare them to be receptive to the CBT, ERP, ACT, or other therapies that they will subsequently try.

Most therapists are leery of trying to engage in spiritual discussions with their clients in general, and especially with scrupulous patients, in particular (for example, CBT, ERP, and ACT do not engage in discussion of the content of one's scrupulous thoughts). There are good reasons for that. One reason is that therapy training programs drill into their therapist trainees that they must be careful not to impose their own personal values (including religious values) onto their clients or patients. Part of being seen as a "professional" is that therapists should avoid lots of personal "folk wisdom," "religious indoctrination," or "advice giving." They try to adopt a more clinical stance using medical terminology and models (like the DSM-5 noted earlier) and stick to secular treatment approaches. In all honesty, there are good reasons for training new therapists to be careful inserting too much of their personal beliefs into their work. Beginning therapy students often fall into the traps I just described above. It takes a sizable degree of professional experience and personal maturity before a therapist is ready to integrate issues of religiosity and spirituality into their professional work at a balanced level. So, it is preferred that new therapists just coming out of graduate school hold off on integrating religious discussions in their clinical work until they are seasoned enough to do so in a balanced way.

Another concern most therapists have about addressing spiritual and religious matters when working with the scrupulous is that they are afraid that focusing on the content of the client's concerns (their religious and spiritual concerns) will only add fuel to the fire and exacerbate the obsessive thoughts and compulsive behaviors. Therapists **correctly** believe that scrupulosity is about the **process** of the mental illness rather than the **content** of their concerns. The treatment of scrupulosity ultimately has to address the patient's mental health processes such as recognizing and relabeling their intrusive thoughts as stemming from their OCD rather than from the Holy Ghost or some spiritual process. Then treatment involves refuting or ignoring those thoughts and impulses without engaging in their typical compulsive behavior, and then finally revaluing or dismissing the obsessive thoughts as not worth paying attention to (i.e. reducing the importance of the thought). So, most therapists want to focus on the processes necessary to ameliorate the OCD symptoms without going into lengthy discussions about the content of their clients' concerns (such as "did I confess properly, were my prayers said meaningfully, or was that behavior I did the other day a sin?"). However, not addressing their clients' spiritual concerns leaves the client feeling alone, unheard, and unsure that they can trust the therapist who is dismissive with something as important as the "salvation of their soul" as the client is still framing the problem. It is necessary to meet the client where they are at to shift them from viewing scrupulosity as a religious concern to a mental health issue. Ignoring the patient's content also leaves untapped the powerful resource that faith can be in overcoming scrupulosity. Particularly, the Restored Gospel of Jesus Christ is replete with comforting truths that can salve the scrupulous soul. It is in understanding the soothing "Balm of Gilead" that the Restored Gospel offers that the sufferer of scrupulosity can begin to take their first steps toward both healthily embracing faith and overcoming scrupulosity. They can turn to God and His servants, as well as competent mental health professionals, as they embrace uplifting Gospel truths and overcome their mental illness. Contrary to most therapists treating scrupulosity, I believe that embracing Gospel truths (specifically the Restored Gospel truths that I will highlight in subsequent chapters) is a key first step to overcoming scrupulosity and healing from this mental illness, before engaging in subsequent phases of treatment involving Mindful CBT, ERP and ACT.

FAITH AS A PRINCIPLE OF ACTION AND POWER IN THE FACE OF UNCERTAINTY

Recent research in OCD has shown that there are at least six "maladaptive OCD-related beliefs" that seem to fuel the flames of the disorder: inflated responsibility, overestimated threat, importance of thought, control of thoughts, perfectionism, and intolerance of uncertainty.[1] Faith can be a powerful principle of action and power in mediating and reducing some of these maladaptive beliefs, especially the latter one – intolerance of uncertainty. Some leading scholars in the field argue that "intolerance of uncertainty" is a "key process in the pathogenesis of scrupulosity."[2] These same scholars urge therapists to move the scrupulous person's religious experiences to become less "fear-based" and more focused on uplifting and encouraging aspects of one's religious life.

Faith is "not to have a perfect knowledge of things" (Alma 32:21), which is very important to remember in the face of uncertainty. Faith is what can hold us on a productive path toward good mental health when we aren't certain. Faith can increase our tolerance for uncertainty until we can get to the other side of the crisis and eventually know the truth of a matter. For the scrupulous, learning to rely on faith rather than certainty can help them stop parsing an issue of anxiety or fear, and let them simply trust in the mercy and goodness of God, take actions recommended by their therapist and church leaders, and believe that their scrupulosity is a mental health issue, not a spiritual malady.

In the *Lectures of Faith* – a compilation of lessons from the School of the Prophets taught by Joseph Smith and others in the Kirtland, Ohio period of the early portion of this dispensation – we read the following marvelous truth:

"...faith is not only the principle of action, but of power, also, in all intelligent beings, whether in heaven, or on earth." *Lecture on Faith* 1:13

Faith is the "moving cause of all action" (*Lectures on Faith* 1:10) and the reason people put forth effort to achieve anything. To paraphrase the teachings on the matter, why would anyone put forth effort to pursue a task – to plant, to invest, to study, to write a book, or to take any action at all – if they did not believe and have faith that their efforts would result in some hoped-for outcome? Faith is therefore motivating. I've often taught the simple conceptual equation: Belief + Action = Faith. When we believe in something so strongly that we are willing to act upon it, then we exemplify faith. So, faith is inseparable from action. We cannot have faith without action. This idea becomes extremely important in Phase III of this model where we use Acceptance and Commitment Therapy or ACT to ameliorate scrupulosity symptoms through predetermined actions. The Epistle of James teaches this truth about faith and action powerfully:

17 Even so faith, if it hath not works, is dead, being alone.

18 Yea, a man may say, Thou hast faith, and I have works: shew me thy faith without thy works, and I will shew thee my faith by my works. – James 2:17-18

Faith is also a principle of power. Faith empowers us to see things that are yet to be – miraculous future possibilities – through combining our efforts and God's grace. When we believe, we can see what can be. When we add action to that faith-filled vision, we can do, become, or bring about whatever God and our hearts desire, which is right.

For the scrupulous, they often "see sin where there is none"³ out of fear and anxiety. Through faith, they can learn to discern between truth and error, trust in God's love and mercy, and hope for good things, which they cannot see at the moment due to their mental health, but which good things are nevertheless true. It's not necessarily a matter of the scrupulous increasing their faith (for they usually have faith in abundance). Rather, it is a matter of *applying* their resilient and resplendent faith toward a new application of their faith. It is having a newfound faith that their souls are not in jeopardy when they feel these anxious impulses, but that their mental health is the issue at hand so they will take the predetermined actions they've established with their therapist and priesthood leaders that they can utilize at such moments to withstand the obsession without relying on their compulsions.

To FURTHER UNDERSCORE the principle of faith as a principle of action and power in the realm of mental health, consider the following verse from the First Lecture on Faith

> "In a word, is there any thing that you would have done, either physical or **mental**, if you had not previously believed? Are not all your exertions, of every kind, dependent on your faith? Or may we not ask, what have you, or what do you possess, which you have not obtained by reason of your faith? ...Reflect, and ask yourselves, if these things are not so. **Turn your thoughts on your own minds**, and see if faith is not the moving cause of all action in yourselves..." *Lectures on Faith* 1:11 (emphasis added).

Since we know that the mental process of OCD (including scrupulosity) starts with a thought in one's mind (an obsession) and then the person acts in a particular way (a compulsion) to try to find emotional relief from the obsession, does not this verse (*Lectures on Faith* 1:11) show that faith can be an intervening variable between the thought and the action? Can we use faith as a way of correcting the obsession (going backwards in the mental process) and then use faith to select an action suggested by their therapist and priesthood leader rather than the previously tried and failed compulsions (going forward in the mental process) that trap the sufferer of scrupulosity? I believe so. I believe that faith in certain foundational truths about mental health and also doctrines of the Restored Gospel of Jesus Christ can be an intervening variable to correct faulty mental notions that grow into obsessions, as well as guide committed, valued actions other than the patterns of compulsions previously tried in moving forward toward overcoming scrupulosity.

So, what are these truths about mental health and the Gospel that the scrupulous can have a more active faith in while tolerating uncertainty? First, the scrupulous must understand that scrupulosity is an anxiety disorder that needs mental health treatment. They've spent their whole life thinking this was a spiritual matter and need to be supported in this new reframe that they are struggling with a mental health issue, not a religious one. They may go back and forth between believing in their old scrupulous mindset that regards their problems as a matter of sin and this new belief that they are struggling with an anxiety disorder. They will need support transitioning their belief in this new cognitive perspective or view of framing the issue as a mental health one. They will also need support framing their views about the nature of God – having faith that He is a loving, rather than punitive God. This must become an active, powerful faith that requires the scrupulous sufferer to change their views and conceptions about God from a legalistic, punishing, harsh force of condemnation into the loving, merciful, and helpful Father in Heaven that He truly is. Such a faith requires that they begin to take *specific actions* (guided by ecclesiastical leaders and therapists) that are different from the compulsions they've tried for years. These new actions are based on new understandings about God and the Gospel, as well as new understandings about how mental health works. I'm talking about a faith that sees the Father and the Savior as Advocates rather than judges (at least in the way we tend to think about judges in the modern day). I'm talking about a powerful, active faith that yields no place for fear, but instead uses faith to push back the fear to a place that can be ignored, dismissed, or at least devalued. That type of faith prompts the struggling soul to not give any heed or credence to the relentless obsessions, and actively place their faith in a loving God who they are beginning to see differently than before and have a more holistic relationship with Him. To heal, the scrupulous soul must also have faith to try the new methods and activities their bishop and therapist are teaching them to do instead of reverting to their compulsive behaviors that only make things worse. That kind of faith includes courage in the face of the fears that won't seem to go away. It's the kind of faith that believes healing from and overcoming scrupulosity is possible even when they only seem to see the doubts and self-incrimination, which linger like mists of darkness on the path to the Tree of Life. And just as the Iron Rod is the word of God that they can cling to during the mists of obsessive doubt, the scrupulous sufferer can cling to the loving, merciful new truths about mental health and about God that are such a different perspective than what they've ever previously felt about Deity before.

The Truth of Things as They Really Are to Defeat "Overestimated Threat"

In Doctrine and Covenants 93:24 we read:

> 24 And truth is knowledge of things as they are, and as they were, and as they are to come;

For the scrupulous sufferer, the idea of truth seems maddeningly elusive. They can see two sides of everything. They are the best at seeing both sides of the argument, but they tend to "hedge their bets" so to speak at guarding against the worst-case scenario – the scenario that is most self-prosecutorial and self-incriminating. That is because they are exceptionally talented at "overestimating threat" (another of the six maladaptive beliefs that fuels OCD). They often have a sharply keen precept of right and wrong and, because they tend to be anxiety prone and risk averse, they want to safeguard against any interpretation that could be used against them. In research terms, they wrestle over the possibility of making either a Type I error (the risk of failing to believe or accept something that is true; i.e. falsely rejecting the truth) or a Type II error (the risk of believing or accepting something as true that is in reality false) about their soul with eternal salvation or damnation hanging in the balance.

Now, if God's nature was one to play cruel jokes on His children, He could leave the struggling person wandering and wallowing in the pit of despair between these two types of errors. But fortunately, that is NOT His nature. He wants us to know the truth about Him and about our standing before Him.

In the April 2018 General Conference, Pres. Russell M. Nelson taught:

> "You don't have to wonder about what is true. (see Moroni 10:5) You do not have to wonder whom you can safely trust. Through personal revelation, you can receive your own witness... Regardless of what others may say or do, no one can ever take away a witness borne to your heart and mind about what is true.
>
> "I urge you to stretch beyond your current spiritual ability to receive personal revelation, for the Lord has promised that 'if thou shalt [seek], thou shalt receive revelation upon revelation, knowledge upon knowledge, that thou mayest know the mysteries and peaceable things—that which bringeth joy, that which bringeth life eternal.' (Doctrine and Covenants 42:61)
>
> "Oh, there is so much more that your Father in Heaven wants you to know. As Elder Neal A. Maxwell taught, 'To those who have eyes to see and ears to hear, it is clear that the Father and the Son are giving away the secrets of the universe!'"[4]

God's orientation towards us is to love us and to reveal the truth to us. He wants us to know Him, and so He is eager to be knowable. God does not want us see Him as a threat, but as an ally who has our best interests at heart. In fact, the scriptures testify that the Savior wants us to clearly know Who and What we worship, how to properly worship God and how to come to the Father through Him. He so taught these very truths in Doctrine and Covenants 93:19:

> 19 I give unto you these sayings that you may understand and know how to worship, and know what you worship, that you may come unto the Father in my name, and in due time receive of his fulness.

Those suffering with scrupulosity struggle to *accurately* know the God that they and we worship. They struggle to know how to properly worship Him and how to live so that they are assured they can return to Him. Learning to stop overestimating God as a threat to their salvation is necessary to overcome scrupulosity. The scrupulous must include faith in the benevolent, redemptive nature of God and His deepest desires and effective efforts to see us successfully return to His presence. The scrupulous must also have faith that through the guidance of their priesthood leader, therapist, and Holy Ghost they can learn "how to worship" God that is neither destructive to their mental health nor salvation. They can rid themselves of compulsive methods of worship and learn to live the Gospel in a healthy and happy way.

Another way of expressing the same sentiment comes from Joseph Smith and others who produced the *Lectures on Faith*:

> "2. Let us here observe that three things are necessary for any rational and intelligent being to exercise faith in God unto life and salvation.
>
> 3. First, the idea that he actually exists;
>
> 4. Secondly, a correct idea of his character, perfections, and attributes;

5. Thirdly, an actual knowledge that the course of life which one is pursuing is according to His will. For without an acquaintance with these three important facts, the faith of every rational being must be imperfect and unproductive. But with this understanding, it can become perfect and fruitful, abounding in righteousness unto the praise and glory of God the Father and the Lord Jesus Christ." (*Lectures on Faith* 3: 2-5).

In essence, the Prophet and others who produced the *Lectures on Faith* are teaching us that the three most important questions everyone has to wrestle with is:

1. Is there a God?
2. What's He like?
3. What does He expect of me, personally? (And how am I doing meeting His expectations of me?)

Those can be excruciating, soul-searching questions for the scrupulous. But they also present the very solution to their problem. Knowing there is a God and knowing what He is really like has tremendous implications for the third question – "How am I doing in fulfilling what He expects of me?" (which is usually at the core of what someone struggling with scrupulosity is wrestling with). If the scrupulous person (who typically does believe that God exists) comes to know the "*correct* idea of (God's) character, perfections, and attributes," then they will be able to have and embrace the powerful, active faith necessary to know what He expects of them and how they are doing in fulfilling God's expectations of them in order to overcome scrupulosity in their lives. To paraphrase Doctrine and Covenants 93:24 in light of the discussion about coming to know who God really is and what He expects of us, the sufferer of scrupulosity must develop the particular kind of active, powerful faith rooted in the principles of the Restored Gospel that helps us to know "God as He is, as He was, and how He will be with us in the eternities." Those all-important truths set a spiritual foundation that is healing and liberating, as well as preparatory for the other therapeutic treatments offered by professional therapists to be more effective.

Fear and Faith

In the October 2008 General Conference, Elder Neil L. Anderson said, "Fear and faith cannot coexist in our hearts at the same time."[5] This is a summary of a statement attributed to Joseph Smith in the *Lectures of Faith*:

> "...For doubt and faith do not exist in the same person at the same time. So that persons whose minds are under doubts and fears cannot have unshaken confidence, and where unshaken confidence is not, there faith is weak..." (*Lectures of Faith* 6:12)

Scrupulosity is often called "The Doubting Disease."[6] Those suffering with this malady are plagued with doubts and fears. One of the crucial initial steps to healing from scrupulosity is learning to differentiate faith from fear. They must come to distinguish the thoughts of doubt and fear as the "voice" of the scrupulosity and the thoughts and feelings that promote faith as coming from God. God does not speak to the scrupulous through their doubts and fears.

One important study[7] concerning perfectionism and scrupulosity among Latter-day Saints found that those saints who focused on a form of perfectionism called maladaptive perfectionism tend to focus on "discrepancy" rather than personal striving to meet standards (adaptive perfectionism) in a healthy way. They suggest that healthy striving to live Gospel standards through adaptive perfectionism manifests a "faith-based approach to religiosity" rather than a "fear-driven" approach to Gospel living borne out of a feeling of discrepancy or "not being good enough." This study found that maladaptive perfectionism was linked to scrupulosity, but adaptive perfectionism was not. Scientific research is finding what the Gospel truths have taught all along – motivations for living righteously are best based in faith rather than fear. Having faith in the goodness of God rather than fearing Him is a healthier approach to religiosity. For the scrupulous, converting their piety from a fear-based (or anxiety-based) emphasis to one that places faith in the goodness of God (and their own goodness) may benefit them.

There a couple of key scriptures each person with scrupulosity should take to heart:

2 Timothy 1:7
7 For God hath not given us the spirit of fear; but of power, and of love, and of a sound mind.

Doctrine and Covenants 6:36
36 Look unto me in every thought; doubt not, fear not.

In the first scripture, the Apostle Paul reminds us that God does not give us the spirit of fear. Scrupulosity speaks to the mind and heart through fear and doubt, but God speaks to us through the Holy Ghost. Communications from the Holy Ghost are designed to deliver God's message in a way that makes perfectly clear to the receiver what God wants him or her to know. God's message doesn't come in shadows and clouds of doubt. Rather, when God wants to communicate with His children He is fully capable of getting the message clearly across. The scrupulous should pray and ask God to speak clearly to them in unmistakable ways so that they do not need to linger in doubt. He powerfully speaks of His love for us. He desires us to have a sound mind, not a mind of doubt or fear. So, for someone struggling with scrupulosity they can have the assurance they need as they distinguish between the voice of fear that comes from scrupulosity or the voice of faith that comes from the Lord.

Furthermore, when the Lord Jesus Christ spoke to Joseph Smith and Oliver Cowdery in Doctrine and Covenants section 6, He commanded them to look to Him in every thought. Then He commands them to not doubt or fear. It is clear that looking to the

Savior in every thought is the opposite of doubting and fearing. Having faith in Jesus Christ does not include the type of doubts and fears that scrupulosity brings. This is a key the sufferer of scrupulosity can use to discern between truth and error. Scrupulosity speaks in doubts and fears; God speaks to empower and encourage faith, hope, and righteousness.

THE DIVINE FOUNDATION of our Faith

For faith to be sufficiently powerful enough to overcome the scourge of scrupulosity, it must be built upon a unique, solid foundation centered in God the Father and His Son. Helaman taught his sons Nephi and Lehi the following:

> 12 And now, my sons, remember, remember that it is upon the rock of our Redeemer, who is Christ, the Son of God, that ye must build your foundation; that when the devil shall send forth his mighty winds, yea, his shafts in the whirlwind, yea, when all his hail and his mighty storm shall beat upon you, it shall have no power over you to drag you down to the gulf of misery and endless wo, because of the rock upon which ye are built, which is a sure foundation, a foundation whereon if men build they cannot fall. (Helaman 5:12)

Heavenly Father and Jesus Christ are the foundation we must build our faith upon. We all must come to know the "only true God, and Jesus Christ" (see John 17:3) and build our foundation on Them. That's one of the reasons I call the first phase of treatment in my approach to treating scrupulosity "Foundational" – because we must first address the spiritual concerns of the person suffering with scrupulosity and establish truths about mental health, the nature of God, and salvation through the Atonement of Jesus Christ as the foundation for all other truths that will bring hope and healing. This Foundational stage (Phase I), focuses on the truth about mental health and the divine nature of God and His Gospel Plan, and is then followed by Phase II Mindful CBT and ERP and Phase III ACT treatments.

When the sufferer of scrupulosity accepts the truth about the mental health nature of their problems and builds their foundation for treatment of scrupulosity on the benevolence and grace of the Rock of our Redeemer, they are building on the very truths that will be a powerful, active force that the sufferer can utilize (with better tools than their compulsions) to heal from the mental health disorder. Once that solid foundation is in place, the other treatments will be more effective.

How does one build this type of faith that can tolerate uncertainty and reduce the estimate of threat from God? It involves a *correct* knowledge of God and His "character, perfections, and attributes" (Lectures on Faith 3:4). Secondly, we must be willing to sacrifice our old ideas and old ways (including the former patterns of responding to obsessions with compulsions) in order to establish newer, healthier ways of responding to troubling, obsessive thoughts, feelings, urges, and impulses. Finally, we must move forward with faith in implementing the new ideas, tools, and strategies that ecclesiastical leaders and therapists will teach to the sufferer of scrupulosity.

Let me further highlight the importance of sacrifice in building faith to overcome scrupulosity. Once again, the Lectures on Faith provide useful understandings:

> "Let us here observe, that a religion that does not require the sacrifice of all things, never has power sufficient to produce the faith necessary unto life and salvation; for from the first existence of man, the faith necessary unto the enjoyment of life and salvation never could be obtained without the sacrifice of all earthly things: it was through this sacrifice, and this only, that God has ordained that men should enjoy eternal life;" *Lectures on Faith 6:7*

For the scrupulous, "enjoyment of life" both in this world and the world to come rests on sacrificing their compulsions and learning to cope with the obsessions in healthier ways. Such sacrifice may be as difficult as Abraham's willingness to offer up Isaac as a sacrifice unto the Lord. But just as the Lord provided an alternative[8*] for Abraham that spared Isaac, the Lord can provide the sufferer of scrupulosity with alternatives that are healthy and more enjoyable than staying with their old compulsions that fail to keep their obsessions in abeyance in the long-run. By sacrificing their compulsions and placing their faith in God and in the new treatment activities recommended by their therapist and Church leaders, they can heal and overcome scrupulosity.

Faith in the three members of the Godhood – the Father, Son, and Holy Ghost – also means having faith in the promptings and messages that we receive through the promptings of the Spirit and from the inspired messages the Spirit gives to the Lord's servants. Having faith in spiritual promptings can be incredibly difficult for those suffering with scrupulosity. Because the impulses, thoughts, feelings, and urges of OCD/scrupulosity can be difficult to distinguish from the thoughts, feelings, and impressions of the Holy Ghost, those with scrupulosity may not be sure which feeling and thought comes from God and which is part of their mental illness. Working with their priesthood leader and therapist, the sufferer of scrupulosity can begin to discern when something is their "OCD talking" and when it is the voice of the Lord. That discernment also comes from practice and experience using the principles distinguishing faith from fear discussed earlier in this chapter. Eventually, the sufferer can place their faith in the promptings of the Spirit. They must also place their faith in the inspired words of prophets, apostles, and other general and local leaders of the Church, but it is important to understand the context of such statements. Knowing when and to whom harsh calls to repentance were directed and when and to whom soft, comforting words of mercy were delivered can help prevent misapplying the counsel. In a general sense, the scrupulous fear getting away with some sin or justifying some impenitent deed more than they seek to harden their hearts against the Lord and His ways. They are not the hard-hearted and stiff-necked sinners deserving of the rebuke and wrath of the Lord. Rather, they are so hard on themselves that they need to begin to place their faith in the comforting words of Christ and His servants that He extends to all those who seek after Him and His ways.

The scrupulous must place their faith in God's mercy rather than in the deceptive brain messages of obsessions, the dead works of compulsions, and the feelings of fear and failure scrupulosity shallowly offers. In Moroni 7:12-19, Mormon teaches his son Moroni how to discern between good and evil, between that which is inspired by God and that which is not. Probably the most succinct summary of the sermon is found in verse 13:

> 13 But behold, that which is of God inviteth and enticeth to do good continually; wherefore, every thing which inviteth and enticeth to do good, and to love God, and to serve him, is inspired of God.

The sufferers of scrupulosity must use this principle to judge between impulses, thoughts, and feelings from scrupulosity and those from God. Does the thought or feeling promote faith, hope, and love? Does it promote compassion for others and one's self? Does it inspire you to serve God? Does it lead you want to do good to others, to serve others, and to serve God? Or does the thought or feeling cause you to turn inward, focus on only your own problems, and foster fear that God won't love or accept you? If the thoughts and feelings are closer to the latter, then the probability is that it is more than likely to be from one's scrupulosity than from God, because that's just not what God inspires people to do. Seeking for and praying for the gift of discernment – as mentioned in Doctrine & Covenants 46:23 – is a righteous goal for the scrupulous so long as they do so in a moderate (non-compulsive) manner. Using the gift of discernment by the Holy Ghost, one can learn to distinguish when a thought or feeling is from God or not.

. . .

Faith vs. A Perfect Knowledge: Intolerance of Uncertainty and The Usefulness of Uncertainty

This brings us back to the issue of uncertainty. In Alma 32: 21-22 we read:

> 21 And now as I said concerning faith—faith is not to have a perfect knowledge of things; therefore if ye have faith ye hope for things which are not seen, which are true.
>
> 22 And now, behold, I say unto you, and I would that ye should remember, that God is merciful unto all who believe on his name...

When we have faith, we hope for true things, but there may be a degree of uncertainty. It is okay to be "mostly believing, but still a little uncertain." Faith allows us to "Doubt your doubts before you doubt your faith."[9] Faith allows us to move forward on our beliefs in spite of any lingering uncertainties without being hypocritical. Even when the sufferer of scrupulosity isn't absolutely sure and doesn't have a "perfect knowledge" about the source of a particular thought or feeling, they can move forward with faith based on the new principles and activities they will learn from their therapist and Church leaders. But it is important to point out that in verse 22 the prophet Alma does make a point of reminding the people he was teaching that in those moments of uncertainty they should remember a core truth about God – that He is "merciful unto all who believe on his name..." When unsure, error on the side of God's mercy is the answer. He is far more perfect in this attribute of mercy than most would possibly believe.

Most therapists will encourage people with any form of OCD, including scrupulosity, to embrace some uncertainty in their lives. It is in parsing an issue to death in search of absolute certainty that the obsessions and ruminations continually feed and thrive. Those with OCD of any kind must starve the obsessions, ignore them, give them no heed, and eventually devalue them as not relevant or important. So, those with OCD must learn to live with the uncertainty for a little while and refocus on other wholesome things for a time even while the OCD-based obsession continues to bother them. Learning to compartmentalize and devalue intrusive thoughts and feelings requires a person to take actions according to their goals and values in spite of the uncertainty.

Living, learning, striving, and yearning amidst the mist of uncertainty is what leads to growth. If we had a certain knowledge every step of the way through life, we would never have to make the hard choices that lead to growth. So, to the scrupulous, I urge them to exercise faith in the midst of uncertainty trusting and hoping in God's mercy. This type of active, powerful faith is a decision that leads to growth. As Neil L. Anderson taught, "Faith is not only a feeling; it is a decision. (We) need to choose faith."[10] Like Nephi, who did "not know the meaning of all things" (1 Nephi 11:17), those suffering with scrupulosity can make a hopeful decision, choose faith, and take powerful action even while "not knowing the meaning of all things." This is essentially taking the posture of humility. In essence, the scrupulous individual choosing this path is deciding to be humble and teachable, accepting the wisdom and counsel of priesthood leaders and their therapist above their own understanding. They are learning to follow the scriptural admonition found in Proverbs 3:5-6:

5 ¶ Trust in the Lord with all thine heart; and lean not unto thine own understanding.

6 In all thy ways acknowledge him, and he shall direct thy paths.

That type of faith and humility is not weakness, but rather meekness. It is a willingness to move forward with faith rather than be immobilized by fear. It is recognizing when we do not know something with certainty, so we choose to move forward with faith rather than be paralyzed by fear. That is one way we grow and overcome the fears and feelings of scrupulosity.

PHASE I: FOUNDATIONAL TRUTHS AND THE GOSPEL OF GROWTH

Good news. That's what the term "gospel" means. It has specific reference to the good news of Christ's atoning triumph over sin and death through His sufferings in Gethsemane and Calvary, as well as His resurrection from the borrowed tomb. In fact, His Atonement is the "best news" we could hope for because it unlocks so many eternal truths and possibilities for us.

The first foundational truth that must be ascertained by the scrupulous is the correct nature of God. They (like all of us) must comprehend His orientation towards us as a perfectly loving and understanding Parent to a developing child. In Jeremiah 29:11-14 we read:

> **11** For I know the thoughts that I think toward you, saith the Lord, thoughts of peace, and not of evil, to give you an expected end.
>
> **12** Then shall ye call upon me, and ye shall go and pray unto me, and I will hearken unto you.
>
> **13** And ye shall seek me, and find me, when ye shall search for me with all your heart.

14 And I will be found of you, saith the Lord: and I will turn away your captivity, and I will gather you from all the nations, and from all the places whither I have driven you, saith the Lord; and I will bring you again into the place whence I caused you to be carried away captive.

God's orientation towards us is to give us peace, rather than evil. He wants to give us the things we hope for and can reliably "expect" from Him as a good and loving Parent. In our seeking and praying, we have the promise that He will make Himself easily findable. In a January 2010 *Ensign* article, one member describes his reflections when the scripture from Jeremiah above was presented in a Sunday School lesson:

"I was reminded of the times when my wife… and I played hide-and-seek with our young children. When it was our turn to hide and their turn to seek, we always made ourselves easy to find. Sometimes we made noises or left a foot in plain view so they would find us quickly. Sometimes we hid in the same place repeatedly. We wanted the children to search for us, but we also wanted them to find us. We looked forward to their hugs and their joyful, unrestrained giggles of triumph.

"This memory deepened my understanding of our Heavenly Father's love for us. He wants us to search for Him, but He also wants us to find Him—He knows how happy we will be when we do. He does not try to trick us. Rather, He does all He can to help us know where and how to search: He gives us the scriptures, calls prophets, listens to our prayers, guides us by the power of the Holy Ghost, blesses us with temples and priesthood ordinances and family and friends. And if we have found Him somewhere once, we are sure to find Him there again if we are willing to renew our search.

"'I will be found of you, saith the Lord.' What a comforting promise! In a world where trouble and temptations seem to find us so easily, it is reassuring to know that our greatest source of strength is so easy to find."[1]

When we understand God's orientation towards us as one of benevolence, peace, mercy, and love in the same way a perfectly good and righteous parent loves their children, then we begin to get a small glimpse of God's nature and desire to bless us.

Elder Jeffrey R. Holland described this orientation and desire God and Christ have towards us in his masterful message "Come Unto Me."[2] This is one of the first of many reading materials I have the sufferer of scrupulosity read when we begin to work in therapy together. I quote from it extensively here, but encourage the reader to study it in its entirety:

> "My desire for you is to have more straightforward experience with the Savior's life and teachings. Perhaps sometimes we come to Christ too obliquely, focusing on structure or methods or elements of Church administration. Those are important and, like the tithes of mint and anise and cummin Christ spoke of (see Matt. 23:23), should be observed—but not without attention to the weightier matters of the kingdom, first and foremost of which is a personal spiritual relationship with Deity, including the Savior, whose kingdom this is.
>
> "The Prophet Joseph Smith taught in the *Lectures on Faith* that it was necessary to have "an acquaintance" (that's his phrase) with the divine attributes of the Father and the Son in order to have faith in them. Specifically, he said that unless we believe Christ to be 'merciful and gracious, slow to anger, long-suffering and full of goodness'—unless we can rely on these unchanging attributes—we will never have the faith necessary to claim the blessings of heaven. If we cannot count on 'the excellency of ... character' (that is also his phrase) maintained by the Savior and his willingness and ability to 'forgive iniquity, transgression, and sin,' we will be, he said, 'in constant doubt of salvation.' But because the Father and the Son are unchangeably 'full of goodness,' then, in the words of the Prophet, such knowledge 'does

away [with] doubt, and makes faith exceedingly strong'" (*Lectures on Faith* [1985], 41–42)...

Elder Holland went on to comment about God's willingness to forgive sins:

"I don't know what things may be troubling you personally, but, even knowing how terrific you are and how faithfully you are living, I would be surprised if someone somewhere weren't troubled by a transgression or the temptation of transgression. To you, wherever you may be, I say, Come unto him and lay down your burden. Let him lift the load. Let him give peace to your soul. Nothing in this world is more burdensome than sin—it is the heaviest cross men and women ever bear.

"The world around us is an increasingly hostile and sinful place. Occasionally that splashes onto us, and perhaps, in the case of a few of you, it may be nearly drowning you. To anyone struggling under the burden of sin, I say again with the Prophet Joseph that God has 'a forgiving disposition' (*Lectures on Faith,*42). You can change. You can be helped. You can be made whole—whatever the problem. All he asks is that you walk away from the darkness and come into the light, his light, with meekness and lowliness of heart. That is at the heart of the gospel. That is the very center of our message. That is the beauty of redemption. Christ has 'borne our griefs, and carried our sorrows,' Isaiah declared, 'and with his stripes we are healed'—if we want to be (Isa. 53:4-5; see also Mosiah 14:4-5)...

"This reliance upon the forgiving, long-suffering, merciful nature of God was taught from before the very foundation of the world. It was always to give us hope and help, a reason to progress and improve, an incentive to lay down our burdens and take up our salvation. May I be bold enough to suggest that it is impossible for anyone who really knows God to doubt his willingness to receive us with open arms in a divine embrace if we will but 'come unto him.' There certainly can and will be plenty of external difficulties in life; nevertheless, the soul that comes unto Christ dwells within a personal fortress, a veritable palace of perfect peace. 'Whoso hearkeneth unto me,' Jehovah says, 'shall dwell safely, and shall be quiet from fear of evil'" (Prov. 1:33)...

Elder Holland continued in his message to expound on how the nature of God and Christ should bring us peace:

"Peace to Our Souls

The Lord has probably spoken enough such comforting words to supply the whole universe, it would seem, and yet we see all around us unhappy Latter-day Saints, worried Latter-day Saints, and gloomy Latter-day Saints into whose troubled hearts not one of these innumerable consoling words seems to be allowed to enter. In fact, I think some of us must have that remnant of Puritan heritage still with us that says it is somehow wrong to be comforted or helped, that we are supposed to be miserable about something.

"Consider, for example, the Savior's benediction upon his disciples even as he moved toward the pain and agony of Gethsemane and Calvary. On that very night, the night of the greatest suffering that has ever taken place in the world or that ever will take place, the Savior said, 'Peace I leave with you, my peace I give unto you. ... Let not your heart be troubled, neither let it be afraid'" (John 14:27).

"I submit to you, that may be one of the Savior's commandments that is, even in the hearts of otherwise faithful Latter-day Saints, almost universally disobeyed; and yet I wonder whether our resistance to this invitation could be any more grievous to the Lord's merciful heart. I can tell you this as a parent: as concerned as I would be if somewhere in their lives one of my children were seriously troubled or unhappy or disobedient, nevertheless I would be infinitely more devastated if I felt that at such a time that child could not trust me to help or thought his or her interest was unimportant to me or unsafe in my care. In that same spirit, I am convinced that none of us can appreciate how deeply it wounds the loving heart of the Savior of the world when he finds that his people do not feel confident in his care or secure in his hands or trust in his commandments.

"Just because God is God, just because Christ is Christ, they cannot do other than care for us and bless us and help us if we will but come unto them, approaching their throne of grace in meekness and lowliness of heart. They can't help but bless us. They have to. It is their nature. That is why Joseph Smith gave those lectures on faith, so we would understand the nature of godliness and in the process have enough confidence to come unto Christ and find peace to our souls. There is not a single loophole or curveball or open trench to fall into for the man or woman who walks the path that Christ walks. When he says, 'Come, follow me' (Luke 18:22), he means that he knows where the quicksand is and where the thorns are and the best way to handle the slippery slope near the summit of our personal mountains. He knows it all, and he knows the way. He is the way.

"Listen to this wonderful passage from President George Q. Cannon teaching precisely this very doctrine: 'No matter how serious the trial, how deep the distress, how great the affliction, [God] will never desert us. He never has, and He never will. He cannot do it. It is not His character [to do so]. He is an unchangeable being; the same yesterday, the same today, and He will be the same throughout the eternal ages to come. We have found that God. We have made Him our friend, by obeying His Gospel; and He will stand by us. We may pass through the fiery furnace; we may pass through deep waters; but we shall not be consumed nor overwhelmed. We shall emerge from all these trials and difficulties the better and purer for them, if we only trust in our God and keep His commandments' ("Freedom of the Saints," in *Collected Discourses*, comp. Brian H. Stuy, 5 vols. [1987–92], 2:185; emphasis added).

"Once we have come unto Christ and found the miracle of his 'covenant of peace,' I think we are under obligation to help others do so, just as Paul said in that verse to the Corinthians—to live as much like he lived as we possibly can and to do as much of what he did in order that others may walk in this same peace and have this same reassurance."

There are several key points to take from this talk by Elder Holland to help overcome scrupulosity:

1. The Lord wants us to have a "personal spiritual relationship with Deity, including the Savior."
2. God's orientation towards us is to be abundantly merciful, gracious, long-suffering, kind, forgiving, loving and "full of goodness." These divine characteristics and attributes of God are in contrast to the way sufferers of scrupulosity view God as a harsh, legalistic Deity focused on punishing us for slight misdeeds, mistakes, and transgressions (which stems from our "Puritan heritage.").
3. God does not want us to be in "constant doubt of salvation," so by understanding God's merciful nature and "forgiving disposition" we can reduce scrupulous anxiety.
4. God wants His children to be happy and have peace, and He is approachable when we need Him.
5. God's character and nature is to bless us, not punish us.
6. There are no loopholes, curveballs, open trenches, or quicksand regarding salvation. Just as one cannot get into heaven on a technicality, we will not be kicked out or excluded on technicalities.
7. We can trust in God during life's difficulties and trials (including mental health challenges) and find reassurance from Him.

Another modern-day apostle, Dieter F. Uchtdorf similarly echoed the same sentiments about the nature of God. While serving as a counselor in the First Presidency, President Uchtdorf said:

"Now, brethren, compared to the perfection of God, we mortals are scarcely more than awkward, faltering toddlers. But our loving Heavenly Father wants us to become more like Him, and, dear brethren, that should be our eternal goal too. God understands that we get there not in an instant but by taking one step at a time.

"I do not believe in a God who would set up rules and commandments only to wait for us to fail so He could punish us. I believe in a Heavenly Father who is loving and caring and who rejoices in our every effort to stand tall and walk toward Him. Even when we stumble, He urges us not to be discouraged—never to give up or flee our allotted field of service—but to take courage, find our faith, and keep trying.

"Our Father in Heaven mentors His children and often sends unseen heavenly help to those who desire to follow the Savior."[3]

In overcoming scrupulosity, members of the Church have the benefit of a "correct idea of (God's) character, perfections, and attributes" from the doctrines of the Restoration.[4] What a marvelous "Balm of Gilead" the Lord offers to the scrupulous sufferer by revealing these truths about His nature through modern-day prophets and apostles!

WHERE DID A "PURITAN HERITAGE" View of God as Harsh, Punishing, and Legalistic Come From?

Professor Terryl Givens, a Neal A. Maxwell Senior Research Fellow at the Maxwell Institute at Brigham Young University and former Professor of Literature and Religion at the University of Richmond, along with his wife, Fiona Givens, have written the book *The Christ Who Heals*,[5] which traces the origins of viewpoints and doctrines that were lost or corrupted during the Great Apostasy and how the Restoration of the Gospel of Jesus Christ in our day restored beautiful truths about God and Christ. The Givens articulately trace the change from the view of God as a loving, nurturing *Father* who aids human growth to an imperial, demanding *"Sovereign"* who negates human will through many early Christian fathers, particularly noting the significant influence of Augustine of Hippo (354-430 AD). They cite a historian of theology, Roger Olson, by stating:

> "Christian theology before Augustine tended to assume a view of God-world relationship called synergism – the idea and belief that God's agency and human agency cooperate in some way to produce... salvation... Pre-Augustinian theologians all assumed that God allowed humans some degree of freedom to make... decisions."[6]

Augustine became the most "influential" figure "between Paul and the Reformation"[7] on shaping and changing Western Christian theology. He wrote prolifically and was responsible for the transformation of views in Christianity that resulted in the concepts of original sin, predestination, and the view of God as the supreme Sovereign who was "less kind and gentle"[8] ordering all things for His benefit rather than for the benefit of humans.

In the Eastern Orthodox Church after the Great Schism, the understanding about Christ's Atonement emphasized sin as a disease that needs to be healed by the Great Physician rather than the Western church's view of sin as a legal violation that needs to be adjudicated by principles of justice and/or mercy.[9] On a parallel, exploring the concept of scrupulosity as a mental illness and anxiety disorder that needs healing (not a sin that needs healing, nor a sin that needs legal adjudication) may be beneficial to those suffering with scrupulosity. Seeing God as a Great Physician healing their mental illness rather than a Sovereign Ruler harshly judging them as a sinner may be an important cognitive shift for the scrupulous in their treatment.

Centuries after Augustine, during the Protestant Reformation, Martin Luther, who most scholars believed suffered from OCD/scrupulosity[10] himself, advanced the notion of God as Sovereign with his argument that salvation comes through the justification by grace through faith in Christ only and that this salvation is completely the work of God alone. As the notion of God as a Sovereign grew, He became increasingly harsh and capricious electing

to do as He would according to His own will and pleasure. Thus, if one was fortunate to have good health or prosperity or cursed to suffer misery and adversity it was solely due to the will of a capricious God. Other Protestant Reformers such as John Bunyan[11] who also suffered from OCD/scrupulosity and John Calvin[12] who had personal anxiety about religious matters, though perhaps not full-blown scrupulosity, further projected their issues onto the conception of God as austere, demanding, and strict.

The culmination of this distorted view of God as harsh and punishing (and of humans as "wicked" souls who should fear Him) could be best summarized by the American preacher Johnathan Edwards' famous sermon *Sinners in the Hands of an Angry God*[13] delivered in 1741 in Connecticut less than a century before the Restoration commenced. Edwards states:

"There is nothing that keeps wicked men, at any one moment, out of hell, but the mere pleasure of God.

"By 'the mere pleasure of God,' I mean his sovereign pleasure, his arbitrary will, restrained by no obligation, hindered by no manner of difficulty, any more than if nothing else but God's mere will had in the least degree, or in any respect whatsoever, any hand in the preservation of wicked men one moment."[14]

In this sermon, Edwards likened humanity to a spider or loathsome insect being held over the fires of hell by a capricious God playing with it:

"The God that holds you over the pit of hell, much as one holds a spider, or some loathsome insect, over the fire, abhors you, and is dreadfully provoked; his wrath towards you burns like fire; he looks upon you as worthy of nothing else, but to be cast into the fire; he is of purer eyes than to bear to have you in his sight; you are ten thousand times so abominable in his eyes as the most hateful venomous serpent is in ours. You have offended him infinitely more than ever a stubborn rebel did his prince: and yet 'tis nothing but his hand that holds you from falling into the fire every moment; 'tis to be ascribed to nothing else, that you did not go to hell the last night; that you was suffered to awake again in this world, after you closed your eyes to sleep: and there is no other reason to be given why you have not dropped into hell since you arose in the morning, but that God's hand has held you up; there is no other reason to be given why you hadn't gone to hell since you have sat here in the house of God, provoking his pure eyes by your sinful wicked manner of attending his solemn worship: yea, there is nothing else that is to be given as a reason why you don't this very moment drop down into hell."[15]

This distorted view of God that sprang from various false doctrines during the Great Apostasy was rampant in the time Joseph Smith. The Restoration of the Gospel through the instrumentality of Joseph Smith corrects this harmful – scrupulosity derived and scrupulosity inducing – view of our Father in Heaven. Yet, too often, Latter-day Saints with scrupulosity may still carry traces of the harsh, punitive God concocted during the Apostasy. Fiona and Terryl Givens explain:

"...the belief that we are all sinners and unworthy of God's love is so seductive that we succumb, unwittingly, to the pervasive doctrines of Augustine... we have drunk so deeply at the Augustinian and Reformation fountains that we are often incapable of either perceiving or savoring the role Christ desires to play in our lives. The vocabulary of sin and guilt and damnation has too often overwhelmed the restored gospel's message of absolute love and powerfully grounded hopefulness. As Elder Neal A. Maxwell said, summarizing the almost universal misapprehension of overanxious Saints among us, we must learn to 'distinguish more clearly between divine discontent and the devil's dissonance, between dissatisfaction with self and disdain for self. We need the first and must shun the second... When conscience calls to us from the next ridge... her purpose is to beckon not to scold.'"[16]

Fiona and Terryl Givens came to the conclusion that since "... Mormonism emerges out of the Protestant world of the nineteenth century, it still bears the influence of that legacy."[17] Fortunately, the Restored Gospel dispels these notions of an austere, exacting, and vindictive God, but the culture that views God as a harsh Sovereign sometimes bleeds into LDS living despite the restored truths. Working with the scrupulous to help them shed the false views of God as a harsh, punishing Sovereign looking to trip them up on some legalistic technicality and embrace the God of Heaven who is our loving Father is essential to healing the disease by which they are bound.

These foundational truths about a loving God are the building blocks upon which healing from scrupulosity can begin. Without knowing and having faith in God's merciful character and orientation towards us, the scrupulous will ever be tortured with the false conception of a harsh, punishing God that they should fear rather than trust. Rather, as Latter-day Saints, we firmly attest that God is interested in our eternal growth and development. A loving, merciful God (who cares more about our growth and development) will be less concerned about the legalistic technicalities that the scrupulous tend to focus on. The scrupulous need to shift their focus to align with God's priorities. If His priorities are about lovingly supporting us in our "eternal goal" of growth, education, and progression, then the sufferer of scrupulosity must shift away from viewing themselves and God through a legalistic-technicality perspective and toward a growth and development perspective.

THE GOSPEL OF GROWTH: **Growing into Godhood**

The famous Christian apologist, C.S. Lewis, made the astute observation about God's view of us as eternally developing and growing beings. In this quote the "He" Lewis references is God and the "them" Lewis refers to is God's children:

"He wants them to learn to walk and must therefore take away His hand; and if only the will to walk is really there He is pleased even with their stumbles."[18]

I learned this truth myself as a young 18-year old man in my freshman year of college. I was privileged to get a scholarship that made it possible for me to attend the University of Southern California (USC) despite my family's financial difficulties. As a result, I attended classes with students whose families of origin were very wealthy, and I was not from the same socio-economic background. I'll never forget parking my rusty 1965 Ford Galaxy (which I borrowed from my parents – complete rust on the panels and duct tape holding parts together) next to several late model BMW, Mercedes Benz, and other luxury cars in the parking structure near the dorms. On campus, it seemed to me like I was a child walking not just among men and women, but men and women who resembled Greek gods and goddesses with their looks, wealth, clothes, and confidence. I felt keenly my "stumbles" as I made mistakes and struggled that year to strive to do well in school and prepare for serving a mission. Many of the Brethren at that time had made comments about how the youth of that generation were among the "noble and great ones" (see Abr. 3:22-23) reserved for the last days. I was miserable, out of my comfort zone, and feeling very lowly and unworthy. I certainly didn't feel very "noble" or "great," but I did believe the prophets and apostles wouldn't lie about such things. I began to privately develop this false idea that I must have been very "noble and great" in the premortal life, but "boy was I really screwing up" down here in mortality. One day, I decided to pray and ask God to give me a glimpse of what I was like in the premortal life so that I could "get a clue" and try to improve here in mortality. The answer to that prayer startled me and changed my life forever. The Spirit told me that I was the same person now (as an 18-year old in mortality) as I was back then (meaning the premortal life) only that I had "grown, developed, and progressed." Those were the words of the Spirit – "grown, developed, and progressed." Knowing that my Heavenly Father didn't see me as a "screw up" despite my sins, foibles, stumbles, and weaknesses, but that I had "grown, developed, and progressed" gave me all the courage and self-confidence I needed. I began to understand repentance, change, and self-worth in a whole new light. I also found that wealth and worldly standards were not the yardstick to judge myself by. I was newly confident in my relationship with my Father in Heaven and that gave me the courage and confidence to serve a mission. My life has been forever changed by viewing myself and others as developmental "works in progress" in an eternal quest to "grow, develop, and progress" towards our heavenly eternal goal.

In the April 2004 General Conference, Elder Bruce C. Hafen of the Seventy spoke about the Gospel plan for mortality as inherently developmental in nature:

"Adam and Eve learned constantly from their often harsh experience. They knew how a troubled family feels. Think of Cain and Abel. Yet because of the Atonement, they could *learn from their experience without being condemned by it.* Christ's sacrifice didn't just erase their choices and return them to an Eden of innocence. That would be a story with no plot and no character growth. His plan is *developmental*—line upon line, step by step, grace for grace.

"So if you have problems in your life, don't assume there is something wrong with you. Struggling with those problems is at the very core of life's purpose. As we draw close to God, He will show us our weaknesses and through them make us wiser, stronger. If you're seeing more of your weaknesses, that just might mean you're moving nearer to God, not farther away."[19]

For the scrupulous, the counsel "don't assume there is something wrong with you" when you are struggling with problems is wise indeed. Because of the developmental nature of God's plan for all of us, we should focus on learning from our experiences rather than feeling condemned by them. Eternal progression is meant to give us hope and joy in the midst of our painful mortal experiences. And perhaps, as Elder Hafen suggests, when the scrupulous see more and more of their weaknesses despite their over-zealous repentance, they can count it as a sign of their growth and drawing closer to God.

Think of sanctification like a series of boulders on a path to godhood that vary from the largest boulder in the first part of the path and gradually smaller ones down the road. As we repent of the larger sins or overcome huge problems that block our view, we move beyond that first ginormous boulder to see another boulder (sins or struggles) that we didn't see before because it was blocked by the first one. It is a little smaller than the first boulder, but with sincere effort and/or repentance we are able to grow or be forgiven and move past the second boulder. We then see a third boulder that was hidden from our view by the first two boulders. But with increased strength and faith in God (and because our previous experiences with repentance gives us greater capacity to repent or overcoming trials gives us greater strength), we repent or grow yet again of the next sin or challenge we were previously unaware of or not focused on. This process goes on and on. Somewhere down the path we may be upset because we find several small stones behind a coconut-sized boulders. Then we may find multiples pebbles behind the small stones. But if we keep striving, the Lord's grace will be sufficient for our sanctification and exaltation (and we will grow in spiritual strength), so long as we keep moving along the covenant path.

SPIRITUAL PERFECTION IS impossible without space to practice, learn, grow, develop, and overcome our mistakes. Could you imagine if we tried to learn to play a new musical instrument, but there was a strict condition that we could never play even one single wrong note or be off pitch in the least? We could never get the fingerings mixed up even once nor could we falter in our getting our embouchure exactly right as we played every single time. Under those conditions, we would never succeed at learning to play a new musical instrument, and frankly, most of us wouldn't even bother to try. But gratefully we accept that it takes practice to learn to play and eventually get things right. Over time, we can learn to play flawlessly the most complicated composition of music. Why? Because the Master Teacher cares more about our personal growth and development, so He allows for forgiveness in the learning process. So it is with life. Because of Jesus Christ's Atonement, we are given space and time in mortality to learn to play the beautiful melody of our lives that God has placed within us. When we sin, make mistakes, or face challenges, He patiently and mercifully forgives us, consoles us, and teaches us how to live in harmony with the tune of righteousness – His great Plan of Happiness. As we learn to trust in His Divine forgiveness, we come to realize we must extend that same forgiveness to others as they learn to play the music of their lives. We often have to endure a wrong note or two from others, but they likewise endure ours. It is in this period of practicing at forgiving others and receiving forgiveness ourselves that we truly grow the most, spiritually. Thus, we have to see sin, repentance, struggle, and forgiveness in a developmental context rather than a static snapshot of the moment.

Human development over an eternity of progression is an exciting prospect and a reality for Latter-day Saints. Viewing our experiences in mortality from a developmental perspective in the context of eternal progression changes how we should understand scrupulosity. If we see life as a fertile environment to experiment and experience the things we need to know, do, and become, to eventually become like God, then we will be able to be more patient with others and ourselves in this trial and error stage of eternity. This mortal existence is the place in our personal, eternal time-frame to try new things (like have a body and learn to master it, or to learn good from evil – and then learn the tougher lesson of good, better, and best[20]). Having an imperfect, mortal body also includes learning how to handle the false brain messages – obsessions – that plague the scrupulous. In the process of growing, we have to try new things and experience new things. No one ever gets everything right the first time. It takes practice, re-dos, falling down, getting back up, learning from our past, and getting things right eventually to grow into the divine beings God wants us to eventually become. Growing into godhood just isn't a mistake-free experience. We can't become like Him without growing, and we can't grow without learning from and repenting of our mistakes. Paradoxically, we must be imperfect to learn from those imperfections how to eventually become perfect. This isn't news to God. He knew all of us (except Jesus) would make mistakes, sin, and fall short of perfection in mortality. Thus, He prepared a plan of salvation that encompassed a mechanism for repentance through the Atonement of His Only Perfect Son whereby His imperfect children could learn, grow, and return back to Him in a more developed, even exalted, state. In fact, the Savior's famous injunction in the Sermon on the Mount to "Be ye therefore perfect, even as your Father which is in heaven is perfect" is all about Christ's invitation to us to grow, develop, and progress thereby being deified just as our Father in Heaven is now deified. The footnote in that verse for the word "perfect" indicates that the meaning of the Greek word *teleios* really means "complete, finished, *fully developed*" (emphasis added on *fully developed*). The idea is that Christ, through His atoning grace, is inviting us to become "fully developed" in the eternities and be like our Father in Heaven. It is a clear statement of the human potential for theosis rather than another tool to critique and to condemn us, as the scrupulous so often do to themselves. Debilitating self-criticism does not aid the path to deification. We should be wary of the critic, especially when it is ourselves.

In 1910, a year after completing his second term as U.S. President, Theodore Roosevelt delivered a speech at the Sorbonne in Paris, France entitled, "Citizenship in a Republic." A famous section of that speech is commonly referred to as the "Man in the Arena" and is an inspiring description of the attitude one should take about trials and errors in the pursuit of growth and goodness:

> "It is not the critic who counts; not the man who points out how the strong man stumbles, or where the doer of deeds could have done them better. The credit belongs to the man who is actually in the arena, whose face is marred by dust and sweat and blood; who strives valiantly; who errs, who comes short again and again, because there is no effort without error and shortcoming; but who does actually strive

to do the deeds; who knows great enthusiasms, the great devotions; who spends himself in a worthy cause; who at the best knows in the end the triumph of high achievement, and who at the worst, if he fails, at least fails while daring greatly, so that his place shall never be with those cold and timid souls who neither know victory nor defeat."[21]

Too often, the scrupulous are their own worst critics. They focus too much on their "stumbles" and where they "could have done better." They do not accurately see that their efforts and valiant strivings with "great enthusiasm" and "great devotions" are commendable and acceptable to God despite their shortcomings. They don't comprehend how in "daring greatly" to grow and live worthily, their vulnerabilities and weaknesses are part and parcel for the course of eternal progression. Trying to live without making any mistakes is antithetical to growth. Learning and growing always involves trial and error. For the scrupulous, the focus is ever on avoiding committing an error, mistake, or sin. For the Latter-day Saint who understands the "Gospel of Growth" perspective, we accept that learning and growing will necessarily stretch us and take us out of our comfort zones. In so doing, we will make mistakes and even sin from time to time. Fortunately, there is repentance where we can correct our ideas and behaviors to align ourselves with God and trust in the merciful Atonement of Jesus Christ on our behalf. We also have a Great Physician to help ameliorate (and sometimes help heal) mental health concerns. We won't be perfect throughout the process, but we will be perfected eventually[22] in the eternities. Until that far off day, we need to "come unto Christ, and be perfected in Him" (see Moroni 10:32) by essentially borrowing on His perfection through the Atonement of Christ. We must learn to trust in His perfection, His Atonement, and His grace, knowing that we will not be perfect in and of ourselves in mortality, but that eventually we will be "made perfect through Jesus the mediator of the new covenant, who wrought out this perfect atonement through the shedding of his own blood" (Doctrine and Covenants 76:69).

THE QUESTIONS THAT HAUNT THE SCRUPULOUS: PERFECTIONISM, SUFFICIENCY IN REPENTANCE THROUGH COVENANT RELATIONSHIPS, AND JUDGING

*P*erfectionism is a plague for the scrupulous. Anything short of perfectionism seems to be cataclysmically catastrophic. The thought that imperfection is a necessary, normative part of the developmental process of becoming divine seems absurd, even blasphemous to most. But Latter-day Saints believe in theosis – the potential for the deification of humanity. Men and women, as children of God, can grow and develop into godhood. The whole point of the plan of salvation is to be exalted – which means to be raised up with our spouses to be like God and be joint heirs with Christ. Of course, He will always rule over us. We could never supplant Him as Satan wanted to do.[1] Our growing glory only adds to His and in no way diminishes it. Andrew Skinner's book *To Become Like God*[2] is an excellent review of LDS doctrine on the subject. But the fact of the matter is that God's mortal children are not yet perfect and He now is perfect in every way. There is a vast chasm separating our imperfection from His perfection. Fortunately, He sent His Son, Jesus Christ – the only person to ever live a sinless life and be perfect in every way. His Atonement is the bridge over the chasm separating our imperfection from God's perfection.

. . .

Adaptive vs. Maladaptive Perfectionism

One of the six maladaptive beliefs that seem to fuel OCD is perfectionism.[3] But it is clear from the research literature that there is a type of perfectionism that is linked with scrupulosity, and a type that is not. Maladaptive perfectionism has a relationship with scrupulosity, whereas adaptive perfectionism does not. What's the difference?

Adaptive perfectionism has several characteristics and has often been called by different descriptors. Adaptive perfectionism seems to focus on the *personal strivings* for high standards or flawlessness, but individuals with adaptive perfectionism are not "necessarily troubled" when those standards are not met.[4] It seems that individuals with adaptive perfectionism understand that striving, but sometimes falling short, is part of the growth process and can accept that growth mindset feature of personal striving for perfection. Adaptive perfectionism seems to be about striving for excellence to please one's self and is therefore self-oriented based on the individual's high standards.[5]

Maladaptive perfectionism, by contrast, is more concerned with what others (including God) think of their efforts, successes, and failures. It is characterized by what researchers call *evaluative concerns*[6] and has a key feature called *discrepancy*, or the feeling of not being good enough.[7] This feeling of not measuring up is particularly concerned with how others will perceive them.[8] Interestingly, those struggling with maladaptive perfectionism and concern about what others think of them have a strong "internal critic" that leads to self-persecutorial (and self-prosecutorial) thought processes. It is as if they are internally seeking to fend off any accusation others (even God) might level at them. This is a form of cognitive distortion where they judge themselves by the harshest criteria.

Two key studies have found a link between adaptive perfectionism, guilt, grace, and a healthy faith-based approach to religious growth and progression as opposed to maladaptive perfectionism, shame, legalism, and scrupulosity (fear or anxiety-based approach to religiosity).[9] Adaptive perfectionism seems to be intrinsically motivated and failures or shortcomings may lead a person to feel guilt.

Guilt is an adaptive emotion that focuses on behavior, not personal identity. It holds us accountable for behaviors, but does not attack our personhood. In contrast, maladaptive perfectionism is motivated by concerns that others will view a person's imperfections pejoratively and, as a result, the person feels shame – that their identity or personhood is deficient in some way (discrepancy). Another way to view it is that adaptive perfectionism fits within a growth mindset, whereas maladaptive perfectionism is locked in a fixed mindset.[10]

Dr. G.E. Kawika Allen and his colleagues studied the relationship between adaptive vs. maladaptive perfectionism, grace vs. legalism, guilt vs. shame, individual and family discrepancy, and healthy religiosity vs. scrupulosity.[11] Their research shows that maladaptive perfectionism and a legalistic view of salvation have a direct link to feelings of shame, as well as a direct link to scrupulosity. Scrupulosity has a link to shame, but that link is further mediated by a sense of family perfectionism and discrepancy (striving to maintain a family with perfect compliance to standards, a concern of what others might think of you and your family, and a feeling of not measuring up).

In contrast, adaptive perfectionism as a means of personal and religious growth with a reliance on God's grace, may lead to behavioral guilt and accountability, but not to scrupulosity or feelings of discrepancy. In other words, when we hold ourselves to high standards because we are personally invested in our individual spiritual growth, but simultaneously recognize our spiritual growth will require some trial and error in life where we are behaviorally accountable (guilt) but reliant on the Savior's atoning grace, we can circumnavigate scrupulosity through such cognitive restructuring. Helping the scrupulous to make these affective and cognitive shifts towards adaptive perfectionism instead of maladaptive perfectionism, growth over a fixed mindset, grace over legalism, guilt over shame, and healthy religious observance over scrupulosity prepares them to better undergo the treatments for scrupulosity found in Phases II and III of this S.O.S. model of treatment.

. . .

Sufficiency in Repentance through Covenant Relationships

Does this mean the scrupulous never need to repent? Well, in a general sense, everyone needs to repent at times in their life, but repentance should be faith-based and not fear or anxiety-based. Repentance should only be for actual sins actually committed intentionally. Most of the time that's not what is going on with the scrupulous. Does having scrupulous feelings, urges, impulses, and obsessions mean the scrupulous have need to repent? Absolutely not! Let me remind you that experiencing scrupulous feelings and urges is a mental health issue, not a spiritual concern. If a person with scrupulosity is feeling urges and impulses to repent, experience has shown they are most likely experiencing an anxiety-disorder, not a bona fide call from God to repent. The scrupulous saint must learn to recognize feelings of dread and urgent impulses to repent or engage in compulsive religious piety as an anxiety-disorder, not an indicator of spiritual or moral failing.

So why discuss repentance at all in a book about scrupulosity? Because it gets at the heart of the legalism/grace issue in the pursuit of healthy adaptive perfectionism studied by Dr. Allen and his colleagues, and because it is a question that often haunts the scrupulous where the answers can ease their concerns and help them feel confident. It also promotes feelings of sufficiency instead of discrepancy.

The scrupulous already know how to repent. They can recite how to repent better than most Latter-day Saints. They have likely thought about repentance more than most. But two aspects usually haunt them – how do they know if they need to repent, and how do they know if they have sufficiently repented?

How does anyone know if they have sufficiently repented? While I don't presume to fully understand how to answer that question for each person, I've learned a few things from my years as a leader in the church and as a therapist that could be useful to ponder on that may help. The one thing for certain is that repentance only works in and through the Atonement of Jesus Christ.

Though I have extensively studied the Atonement of Jesus Christ, I cannot pretend to know how it exactly works – but I know that it does![12] The infinite nature of the Atonement of Christ is not completely fathomable to my finite mind. That's why I find analogies so helpful.

One of the first analogies I discovered years ago while serving as a missionary that helped me understand the Atonement was from BYU professor Stephen Robinson's book *Believing Christ*[13]. He outlined two analogies about the Savior's Atonement that made so much sense to me: 1. "The Parable of the Bicycle" and 2. His financial status when he married his wife.

While his "Parable of the Bicycle" whereby he intervened to buy a bicycle for his daughter after her best efforts to save up for it were woefully inadequate is a well-known story, the lesser-known parable about his financial status when he married is what I'd like to focus on. Dr. Robinson noted that when he was about to get married to his wife, he had debt. To use a bookkeeper's term, he was "in the red." His wife-to-be, however, was not in debt. In fact, she had some assets – more assets than he had debts. So, even though he was individually in debt or "in the red," her assets were enough that when they entered into the covenant relationship of marriage *together* they were "in the black" (meaning still having money left over even after his debts were paid). He compared that to the Savior's Atonement. When we sin, we incur spiritual debt. Sin causes us to be "in the red" and we are not sufficiently capable to pay that spiritual debt in and of ourselves. But when we are baptized we enter into a very sacred covenant relationship with the Savior – the kind of close, connected relationship that the only other human relationship we can compare it to is marriage (though even the marriage analogy is insufficient to fully capture the power and connection of our sacred, covenant relationship with the Lord). Because of the Atonement of Jesus Christ, He has spiritual assets. When He suffered in Gethsemane He paid the price of our sins, and then paid them again while suffering on the cross.[14] It is clear that He didn't just barely pay the price that Elder Neal A. Maxwell called the "awful arithmetic of the atonement,"[15] rather, Jesus amply and abundantly paid the price of every sin, sickness, frailty, and human misery so much that the bitter cup freely overflowed. Christ, through the Atonement, has more than enough spiritual assets to outweigh our spiritual debts. When we enter into this covenant relationship with Him, our spiritual debts are covered and resolved through His spiritual assets. By ourselves, we are spiritually "in the red," but with our covenant relationship with Christ *together* we are spiritually "in the black" or "perfected in Christ" (Moroni 10: 32-33) and "fitted for heaven"[16] that we may be reconciled with the Father and dwell eternally in His kingdom.

From this idea of our covenant relationship with Christ being compared to a marriage analogy, we can then symbolically understand many things about the Atonement. Obviously, we are not literally married to Jesus (just like the Sacrament of the Lord's Supper is not literally the body and blood of Christ, the marriage analogy between Christ and members of the Church is symbolic and figurative). The symbolism of the Christ's Atonement can teach us how deeply and permanently the Savior loves us. We can learn that we don't have to do things all on our own – that salvation can't be achieved on our own but only as we have faith in the Lord and work in concert with the Redeemer to qualify for His grace. And we can learn why He'll never give up on us as long as we don't give up on ourselves, among others. Perhaps it is because I'm a marriage and family therapist that I find the marriage analogy of redemption through our covenant relationship with Christ so illuminating.

One example I often use in counseling others about the Atonement of Christ is the "Parable of the Socks and the Laundry Hamper."

THERE WAS ONCE a man married to a lovely wife. They had a great marriage in many respects, but one issue arose early in their married life. The husband had a propensity to take off his dirty socks and "shoot baskets" with those socks toward the hamper across the room. The problem was that he wasn't as good of a shot as he thought he was, and (more often than not) the socks ended up on the floor near the hamper rather than in it. He also wasn't the conscientious type to go over and pick up the socks on the floor when he missed making the basket. He just left them there on the floor near the hamper. His loving wife was kind, but firm in her boundaries. She didn't mind washing the clothes in the hamper, but she wasn't about to be her husband's "maid" and pick up his scattered dirty socks when he missed making a basket into the hamper. She asked him to please pick up his own dirty socks so they would be in the hamper and not on the floor.

Well, the husband honestly tried for a while to be mindful of his wife's wishes and tried to be considerate about getting his dirty socks into the hamper. But human nature being what it is, he was "foolish and unstable" in his determination to please his wife, and he eventually fell back into the habit of shooting baskets with his socks and leaving the missed ones on the floor.

What would you imagine the wife did in response? Did she divorce him? No, of course not. Instead she firmly reminded him of his promise not to shoot baskets with his socks and leave them on the floor. Essentially, she "chastened him" and "called him to repentance." The husband responded penitently by promising not to do that again. Harmony in their marital relationship was restored. This went on for an even longer period of time where the husband ensured the dirty socks were in the hamper, but eventually the natural man within himself got the best of him and he "relapsed" into his old sock-shooting behavior. The wife once again was patient. Rather than divorce him, she once again chastened him and he repented of his ways. The cycle of behaving by ensuring the dirty socks were in the hamper followed by lapses, chastening, and repentance went on for many years. Despite the seriously irksome behavior of the husband's wayward sock-shooting, the wife never left him. Sure, there were times of relational discord, but they always worked it out as the husband sincerely repented.

One day something very significant happened. The husband was about to shoot baskets with his dirty socks and before he did so, with the help of the Holy Ghost, a few thoughts instantaneously popped into his mind. He first pictured his wife who was very pregnant with their fourth child having to bend over and pick up his socks. Despite her physical difficulty at having to bend over the large swelling in her abdomen due to the baby inside her, she picked up the socks anyway out of love for her husband and a desire to have a clean house. The second thought was of his three-year-old son watching dad shoot baskets and then mimicking dad's behavior with his own little *socks – leaving them on the floor for mom to pick up. The third thought was of the area of the room near the hamper covered with a mountain of smelly, dirty socks piled up against the hamper and knew that if it weren't for his wife, the room would be an unpleasant mess. He realized in that moment that he really did value a clean room and should act accordingly. He actually did want a clean room in and of himself, not just because that was what his wife liked. Secondly, he realized what a poor example he had set for his children and how they were not learning to be responsible. Finally, he came to understand the great burden he placed on his wife through his thoughtless actions, how she'd been patient with his carelessness, how much she loved him that she would labor to keep the room clean, and also that she loved him enough to not enable him, but rather to have high expectations that he repent and change his ways. In that moment, he wanted the socks in the hamper as much as his lovely wife did and he changed his behavior to fit his new value. The couple never again had a problem with socks being left outside the hamper ever again.*

TAKEN TOGETHER, Brother Robinson's parable about "marital finances" and my parable about socks and the laundry hamper underscore a pivotal point – it is the "covenant relationship" we have with Jesus Christ that saves us. That covenant relationship is often symbolized in the scriptures as a marriage.[17] After we have entered into these sacred covenants with the Savior through baptism and ensuing ordinances, we take upon ourselves His name, become part of His family and the Church of the Firstborn, and are redeemed through the righteousness of the Redeemer.

At a BYU Women's Conference on May 4, 2018, the newly called apostle, Elder Gerritt W. Gong, described a concept of ministering to others called "covenant belonging."[18] In a Deseret News article, it was reported that Elder Gong expressed the following ideas:

> "In the revelation of our true, divine selves through our covenants with God we learn to recognize and love our brothers and sisters as He does. This deepening love and knowledge invites, empowers and

sanctifies us to know and, in our own way, to become more like Him...

"There is divine harmony and resonance in covenant belonging as we are strengthened in His love and as we strengthen each other in the Lord...

"We belong to each other. By divine covenant, we belong to God and to each other. Covenant belonging is a miracle. It is not possessive. It 'suffereth long, and is kind.' It envieth not, vaunteth not itself, is not puffed up. Covenant belonging gives roots and wings. It liberates through commitment. It enlarges through love.

"In covenant belonging, we strengthen each other in His love, thereby coming more to love God and each other."[19]

This concept of "covenant belonging" is very applicable to aiding the sufferer of scrupulosity to understand their relationship with God and His grace. We all belong to God. We are His children. But as Latter-day Saints, we also belong to God (and He to us) in a very unique way beyond the level of common humanity – we are connected to God through covenant relationships. Through the ordinances of baptism, confirmation, and other ensuing essential ordinances, we are bound to God – and He to us – in a very personal, individual, and intimate way. It is this covenant relationship that delivers us from sin and spiritual death. Repentance is how we maintain a good covenant relationship with the Lord.

In the scriptures, whenever God was about to initiate a sacred covenant with one of His prophets, there always seems to be a salutary introduction where He introduces Himself by name and calls upon the prophet by name. For a few examples, notice the following verses:

<u>Commencement of the Abrahamic Covenant</u>
Abraham 1:16

16 And his voice was unto me: Abraham, Abraham, behold, my name is Jehovah, and I have heard thee, and have come down to deliver thee...

. . .

ABRAHAM 2:8

8 My name is Jehovah, and I know the end from the beginning; therefore my hand shall be over thee.

<u>NEPHI RECEIVING</u> the Sealing Powers of the Priesthood
Helaman 10:6

6 Behold, thou art Nephi, and I am God. Behold, I declare it unto thee in the presence of mine angels, that ye shall have power over this people

<u>JOSEPH SMITH</u> and the Commencement of the Restoration
Joseph Smith – History :17

17 ...When the light rested upon me I saw two Personages, whose brightness and glory defy all description, standing above me in the air. One of them spake unto me, calling me by name and said, pointing to the other—*This is My Beloved Son. Hear Him!*

SIMILAR EXPERIENCES CAN BE FOUND in the calling of Jeremiah, Isaiah, Enoch, Samuel, Moses, and others.[20] In each example, it is as if the Lord calls the prophet by name and says, "I know you and you know me. We are bound together by covenant. Through this covenant relationship you shall be saved and miraculous things shall be accomplished."

It is our covenant relationship with Christ that saves us. He is our Mediator and Advocate with the Father (see 2 Nephi 2: 27-28 and Doctrine and Covenants 45:3-5). Through the Savior's "perfect atonement," good and just men and women are "made perfect" through the "new covenant" He makes between God and us as the Mediator on our behalf (Doctrine and Covenants 76:69). The scriptural evidence is clear that we are saved through the "new covenant" Christ makes with humanity (see 1 Tim. 2:5, Heb. 8:6, Heb. 9:15, Heb. 12:24, Doctrine and Covenants 107:19 and Doctrine and Covenants 76:50-70).

By learning to trust in one's covenants with God through Christ, the scrupulous can overcome the fear of imperfection. As President Russell M. Nelson taught, perfection is "pending"[21] and will not be achieved in mortality. He notes that even the Savior – though perfectly sinless His whole life – didn't include Himself as perfect until He had a perfected, resurrected, and glorified body.[22] Perfection happens "eventually"[23] in the eternities. Until then, the Atonement of Christ "covers"[24] us as we borrow Christ's perfection and are "perfected in Him" (Moroni 10:32). Our responsibility is to maintain a good covenant relationship with Christ through our continual efforts and repentance, but it is not our works that saves us. Our "works" help us grow, develop, and progress (and therefore have an important role in our exalting progression), but they do not save us. Rather, it is the grace of Christ that saves us through the covenant relationship we establish and maintain with Him. Our part is to "keep on the covenant path"[25] that President Russell M. Nelson frequently speaks of. Keeping on the covenant path includes keeping our covenant relationship with God in good order, but we will never be perfect in all that we do. Elder Gerrit W. Gong reminds us to "remember perfection is in Christ, not in ourselves or in the perfectionism of the world."[26] He goes on to advise those who are burdened with feelings of inadequacy, uncertainty, or unworthiness to trust in the grace of Christ and that His grace is *sufficient* for them:

> "God's invitations are full of love and possibility because Jesus Christ is 'the way, the truth, and the life.' To those who feel burdened, He invites, 'Come unto me,' and to those who come to Him, He promises, 'I will give you rest.' 'Come unto Christ, and be perfected in him, ... love God with all your might, mind and strength, then is his grace sufficient for you, that by his grace ye may be perfect in Christ.'
>
> "In this assurance 'by his grace ye may be perfect in Christ' is also the comfort, peace, and promise that we can continue forward with faith and confidence in the Lord even when things do not go as we hope, expect, or perhaps deserve, through no fault of our own, even after we have done our best.

"In various times and ways, we all feel inadequate, uncertain, perhaps unworthy. Yet in our faithful efforts to love God and to minister to our neighbor, we may feel God's love and needed inspiration for their and our lives in new and holier ways."[27]

For most people suffering with scrupulosity, it is not that they are reticent or recalcitrant to repent. Rather, most scrupulous souls fear their repentance is insufficient or imperfect. In their quest for perfectionism, they seek perfection in repentance. Elder Gerrit W. Gong wise counsel to avoid relying on perfectionism in ourselves and the "perfectionism of the world"[28] seems to apply to the scrupulous in their quest for perfectionism in repentance. Just as imperfection in other areas of living the Gospel is a condition of mortality, so it may be with repentance.

Repentance[29] is not a checklist that if a miniscule detail is done clumsily, the whole process is invalidated. Elder David A. Bednar recently counseled against a focus on checklists in our spiritual growth:

"Sometimes as members of the Church we segment, separate, and apply the gospel in our lives by creating lengthy checklists of individual topics to study and tasks to accomplish. But such an approach potentially can constrain our understanding and vision. We must be careful because pharisaical focus upon checklists can divert us from drawing closer to the Lord."[30]

The goal of repentance is a change of heart and behavior. Repentance should bring us closer to God, not place a further wedge between us and God. Pharisaical checklists involve scrutinizing the letter of the law and ignoring the spirit of it. Repentance should be transformational and exalting – an opportunity to align ourselves with God and our divine nature rather than another source of shame. In working with a woman suffering from scrupulosity, I told her the difference between guilt and shame is that guilt or godly sorrow focuses on changing and improving behaviors, but shame is about feeling awful about our identity and personhood. Repentance involves guilt, but not shame because our identity as a child of God full of infinite worth is set and immovable. Our behaviors may or may not be consistent with our identity. When our behaviors fall short of our divinely appointed identity, repentance is how we align our behaviors to match our identity as children of God so that we can grow into the full measure for which we were created.

This developmental perspective of the Gospel as emphasizing growth and individual (and family) progression rather than shame has important implications for how we view repentance. In the April 2019 General Priesthood Session of General Conference, Pres. Nelson emphasized this shift in our perspective of repentance from one of punishment to growth:

> "Too many people consider repentance as punishment—something to be avoided except in the most serious circumstances. But this feeling of being penalized is engendered by Satan. He tries to block us from looking to Jesus Christ, who stands with open arms, hoping and willing to heal, forgive, cleanse, strengthen, purify, and sanctify us.
>
> "The word for *repentance* in the Greek New Testament is *metanoeo*. The prefix *meta-* means "change." The suffix *-noeo* is related to Greek words that mean 'mind,' 'knowledge,' 'spirit,' and 'breath.'
>
> "Thus, when Jesus asks you and me to "repent," He is inviting us to change our mind, our knowledge, our spirit—even the way we breathe. He is asking us to change the way we love, think, serve, spend our time, treat our wives, teach our children, and even care for our bodies.
>
> "Nothing is more liberating, more ennobling, or more crucial to our individual progression than is a regular, daily focus on repentance. Repentance is not an event; it is a process. It is the key to happiness and peace of mind. When coupled with faith, repentance opens our access to the power of the Atonement of Jesus Christ."[31]

Rather than viewing repentance as a checklist which must be

followed perfectly (which is how the scrupulous often view repentance), the scriptures command us to "bring forth therefore fruits worthy of repentance..." or "fruit meet for repentance" (see Luke 3:8, Alma 12:15, Alma 13:13, and Alma 34:30). In other words, our repentance should be sufficient, meet, or worthy of the Lord's forgiveness in such a way that is fortuitous for our growth and eternal progression. The Lord is the one who determines when our repentance is sufficient to obtain forgiveness. In Mosiah 4:19-20, King Benjamin reminds us we are "all beggars" who are "begging for a remission of (our) sins." Beggars do not determine the sufficiency of their efforts to obtain their desired outcome – the giver of the gift determines that. The sufficiency of repentance is determined by the Lord – the Giver of grace and forgiveness – and His servants, not the penitent. His requirements are clear. He requires us to have a "broken heart and a contrite spirit" (3 Nephi 9:20) and that we repent and return unto Him "with full purpose of heart" (3 Nephi 10:6). It is truly a matter of sincerity of the penitent heart for the Lord, not pharisaical obedience to checklists that brings forgiveness. If the scrupulous person's confessions, prayers, and contrition are sincerely penitent but humanly flawed by their mortal frailties or mental illness, the Lord understands and is merciful. He compassionately inspires His bishops, stake presidents, and other judges in Israel what the penitent needs to do to bring forth "fruits" – actions, prayers, confession, and contrition – sufficient to obtain the Lord's forgiveness. The Lord seems to take into account the intentions of our heart, the level of accountability, the level of Gospel maturity, a person's mental health, and other developmental factors when considering when repentance is sufficient to warrant His forgiveness. Repentance is about turning away from sin and turning toward God so that we can grow and become like Him – not a pharisaical checklist rivaling the worst bureaucratic procedural format only conceivable in the personal, hellish mental processes of the scrupulous mind. No, repentance, rather, is a gift of grace from a loving Heavenly Father made possible through His equally loving Son extended to us in kindness aimed at developing us into our best selves. Repentance comes by way of invitation to exaltation, not the fear of condemnation into damnation.

Now let me be clear – when I speak of repentance by those sincerely seeking to do their best to repent that is inadvertently imperfect or flawed in some way but nevertheless sufficient in the eyes of the Lord, I am not suggesting a lackadaisical, casual, or laisse faire approach to repentance where one half-heartedly repents or skips important elements out of fear, laziness, or embarrassment. I'm not talking about skipping confession of sins to a bishop altogether out of embarrassment nor of choosing to forego some other necessary portion of the repentance process to make things right with God and our fellowman because we simply don't feel like doing so. No, when I speak of flawed, but sufficient repentance, I am talking about someone who truly seeks to do his or her all to fully repent to the best of their ability, but their capacity to do so is imperfect given our mortal conditions. Maybe restitution isn't fully possible or would be more detrimental to others. Maybe the scrupulous confessed their sins as forthrightly as possible at the time, but remembered some minutia about the sin that they aren't sure they communicated clearly *enough* to the bishop, so they want to go in and confess over and over again to the same sin due to the anxiety relief a confession compulsion brings, even though their confessional addendums add no substantive value to their original confession. Sometimes the scrupulous aren't sure whether or not a particular sin requires confession to a bishop or can just be repented of between themselves and the Lord. That is a matter that the bishop and the penitent can talk about and discuss privately from the onset of their relationship, whereby the priesthood key holder can outline for the penitent person what types of sins would put Church membership into question and would require a confession to a judge in Israel and what things may be repented of without involving priesthood leaders as outlined in the Church Handbook of Instructions. Then the scrupulous should follow the guidelines specified by their priesthood leader and only confess when such sins meet the criteria the priesthood leader outlines.

Perhaps the person repenting is developmentally not capable of fully understanding the magnitude of the sin at the time of their repentance. For example, while I was serving as a bishop, I had a 13-year old young man come in to confess a very serious moral transgression of the law of chastity. I worked with him for months. He had confessed the sin and forsaken it (see Doctrine and Covenants 58: 42-43) but I worried his remorse and comprehension of the magnitude of the sin where somewhat shallow. I counseled with my stake president concerning the matter and he told me that he is a 13-year old boy with a 13-year old understanding of sin and repentance. That was the best the boy could do, to accept him at his level of development, and help him move forward by serving in the Gospel. That's what we did. His sacrament and priesthood restrictions were removed and he began serving faithfully in the priesthood once more. Now, suppose that the 13-year old boy grows up and a decade or two later better understands to a greater degree the gravity of his sin from his youth and feels deeper sorrow. Should he feel the need to go and confess and repent all over again with his new level of spiritual awareness? Of course not. He was forgiven by the Lord and the Church for his repentance at his *developmental capacity at the time.*

Too often, people with scrupulosity, engage in this type of re-visitation of prior sins that they repented of a long time ago, but now feel more remorse for because they have grown spiritually. There is no need to go back and "re-repent" after one has repented to the best of their ability at the time. If they did as instructed by their priesthood leader and acted with sincerity and good faith, then their repentance is sufficient. Even if some element of repentance, in retrospect, was flawed somehow, if they did "confess and forsake" the sin as Doctrine and Covenants 58:42-43 directs and their priesthood leader has cleared them to resume their spiritual duties in the Church, they should let go of the guilt from the sin and move forward. I encourage people with scrupulosity who intend to confess to a priesthood leader some new sin to pray for the Lord's help to "honestly and fully confess" the first time, and then, when new thoughts or doubts concerning the confession arise (and they will for the scrupulous), to have faith in their original prayer and trust that they did their best *at the time in their developmental capacity* and then trust in God's grace if there was any imperfection in their repentance. If they sincerely strove to confess everything, there is no good that will come from subsequent amendments to their original confession. They need to focus on forsaking the sin at that point and then serve the Lord and others in positive ways. To linger on ruminations of remorse is to rob or sap strength from their future required service to God and others.

Another frequent concern about repentance not perfectly completed in checklist fashion is whether or not one's restitution is sufficient. For some matters, restitution is clear – if you stole a candy bar from a store, tell the store owner what you did and pay for it. But other cases of restitution aren't always as clear. Maybe restitution isn't possible in certain situations. For example, once one has engaged in sexual activity with another, you can't easily make restitution. You can't "undo" having sex with someone. It's not like a stolen candy bar that can simply be repaid. But if the sincerely repentant person wants to make restitution for sexual sin, maybe in the future when they are a parent, a youth leader, or in some other capacity, they can help influence a youth to make wiser choices concerning sexual purity when they are faced with temptation. It is somewhat like the concept of "paying it forward" rather than "paying it back." That kind of restitution often comes long after the Lord has forgiven the person. The person need not suppose the Lord hasn't forgiven them because the opportunity to be an "influence for good" type of restitution experience hasn't yet happened. Rather, they must trust in the Lord's forgiving grace, accept the remission of their sins He offers, and then look for positive ways to serve both now and in the future. The point is that people suffering with scrupulosity must stop trying to judge themselves and their imperfections so harshly. Such legalistic judgements often get in the way of spiritual growth and progression which is entirely the whole point of the Plan of Salvation – to grow us into godhood. Instead, we must learn what the Lord means by the words "judge" and "judgment" and apply those lessons to ourselves so that we can grow in the light of the Lord and in His goodness.

. . .

JUDGES AND JUDGING: Christ as Our Advocate

A few months before I was called as the bishop of the new Yosemite Ward in the Fresno West Stake, I was in the Fresno Temple completing an endowment session prior to a stake meeting planned for later that evening. I was serving on the High Council at the time, and we were meeting later that evening with our Area Authority Seventy where the theme of the meeting was to be 3 Nephi 27:27 which reads:

> 27 And know ye that ye shall be judges of this people, according to the judgment which I shall give unto you, which shall be just. Therefore, what manner of men ought ye to be? Verily I say unto you, even as I am.

As I sat there in the Celestial room reading that verse, I felt the Spirit overwhelmingly impress upon me the adapted thought from the beginning of that verse: "Know ye not that ye shall be the judge of this people?" The Spirit was telling me that the Lord intended to call me to be the bishop – a "judge in Israel" – of the new Yosemite ward we had been discussing creating in the stake. The Stake Presidency and High Council had been discussing merging my home ward at the time (Coarsegold Ward) with the smaller neighboring ward (Oakhurst Ward) where I was the High Council adviser and calling the new unit the Yosemite Ward. It felt almost as if the Lord was saying, "Duh. Don't you get it? You've been working on this ward combination assignment with the Stake Presidency for months. I intend to call you to be the bishop of the new ward, so pay attention and focus on what manner of men you're supposed to be – even as the Savior is." Talk about a spiritual wakeup call!

For the next few months I felt odd every time I thought about that impression. I didn't want to aspire to anything in the Church, but the impression was so strong I couldn't shake it for months. When the Stake Presidency did extend the call to me to serve as bishop of the ward, it almost felt like a relief – that I wasn't crazy or aspiring to anything – rather, that the Lord was preparing me.

That experience of serving as a bishop – a judge in Israel – got me curious about what the Lord means to be a judge "even as (Christ) is." How does the Savior judge us? What does He do in His role as the "Great and Eternal Judge" at the last day? What can we learn from all of the judges in Israel – from the Book of Judges to our modern-day judges in Israel? What Hebraic concepts about judges and judgment can shed light on this subject?

The result of that inquiry has potentially tremendous benefits and application to the people suffering with scrupulosity. As we will see, the Savior's judicial concept is very different from the world's viewpoint. Rather than being a harsh, legalistic punishing judge, the Savior's idea of judgment and being a judge in Israel has more to do with actively advocating, delivering, rescuing, and redeeming than it does with condemning.

There are two main root words for "judge" in the Hebrew language. One is "Shofet" and the other "Dayan" (or sometimes just "dan" or "din"). While the English translations of the bible translate both of them as the word "judge," there are different subtleties and nuances that distinguish the two terms. The title "Shofet" seems to convey a sense of leadership or ruler. In this sense the "judges" in the Book of Judges (like Deborah, Gideon, and Samson) were more like tribal leaders and warriors who meted out justice by leading Israel into battle against their enemies and saving them from probable defeat. They didn't sit back and wait for cases to be brought to them to make harsh judgements and distinctions all the while interpreting and pontificating from a bench in some court of law. Rather, they were actively out leading the people and seeking ways to bring about their deliverance from their enemies. Other translations for "shofet" have been "general,"[32] someone with "personal charisma,"[33] "deliverer,"[34] and "rescuer."[35]

"Dayan" tends to refer to the position of a judge who has studied the law and metes out justice according to his understanding of the law. The modern-day position of a "Dayan" in contemporary Jewish culture is more akin to what we think about as a judge in our secular courts, but there is a key difference in the ancient[36] sense of judges and judgement in Hebrew culture with the root words "din" or "dan" that make them more broadly used like the root "shofet." "Din" or "dan" was used anciently to signify someone with natural ability to lead and bring about justice through being helpful in providing deliverance to the oppressed.[37] For example, the name "Daniel" is usually interpreted as "God is my Judge"[38] but can alternatively be interpreted more broadly as "God is my Salvation"[39] because of the Hebrew understanding that God's judgement should lead to salvation or deliverance of the oppressed from the wicked.[40]

Some Old Testament scriptures that convey this Hebraic idea of a judge being a deliverer, rescuer, or savior who brings justice and redemption to the oppressed include:

JUDGES 2:16 (emphasis added)
16 ¶ Nevertheless the Lord raised up *judges*, which *delivered* them out of the hand of those that spoiled them

GEN. 30:6 (emphasis added)
6 And Rachel said, **God hath judged me**, and hath also heard my voice, and hath given me a son: therefore called she his name **Dan**.

PSALMS 72: 2-14 (emphasis added)
2 He shall *judge* thy people with *righteousness*, and thy poor with judgment.
3 The mountains shall bring peace to the people, and the little hills, by righteousness.
4 He shall *judge the poor of the people*, he shall *save* the children of the *needy*, and shall *break* in pieces *the oppressor*.

ISAIAH 3:13 (emphasis added)

13 The Lord standeth up to *plead*, and standeth to *judge* the people.

WHILE THERE IS no way to know for certain which form of the word judge (shofet or dan/dayan) the Savior used in the scripture 3 Nephi 27:27 about being the same type of judge that He is (because the Book of Mormon's original manuscripts the Church has are in English and the Reformed Egyptian on the plates would not likely convey the Hebrew root words if we had the plates to study anyway), it doesn't really matter. Both forms of the word "judge" in Hebrew convey a person who is expected to not only mete out justice, but is also to *actively* seek to save, rescue, and deliver the Lord's people – particularly those who are poor, oppressed, or suffering. So, we need to begin to see the Savior in His role as "Judge" as one who is actively seeking to save, rescue, deliver, plead for, and advocate for us rather than condemn us. He, himself, declares to us that He is our Advocate with the Father pleading for us on our behalf during our day of judgment:

Doctrine and Covenants 45:3-5

> 3 Listen to him who is the advocate with the Father, who is pleading your cause before him—
>
> 4 Saying: Father, behold the sufferings and death of him who did no sin, in whom thou wast well pleased; behold the blood of thy Son which was shed, the blood of him whom thou gavest that thyself might be glorified;
>
> 5 Wherefore, Father, spare these my brethren that believe on my name, that they may come unto me and have everlasting life.

Notice how nowhere in that verse does the Savior say to the Father, "Look how perfectly they repented. They checked off every single step of repentance perfectly, so I guess we have to (begrudgingly) let them in." Rather, the Savior requests His Father "spare" us and grant us "everlasting life" because of what He, the Messiah, did – because of His Atoning suffering and our covenant relationship as "brethren" who believe on His name.

This idea about the Savior's form of judgment being one oriented towards deliverance and salvation brings a new understanding to the words of Isaiah found in the scripture 2 Nephi 6:16-18

> 16 For shall the prey be taken from the mighty, or the lawful captive delivered?
>
> 17 But thus saith the Lord: Even the captives of the mighty shall be taken away, and the prey of the terrible shall be delivered; for the Mighty God shall deliver his covenant people. For thus saith the Lord: I will contend with them that contendeth with thee—
>
> 18 And I will feed them that oppress thee, with their own flesh; and they shall be drunken with their own blood as with sweet wine; and all flesh shall know that I the Lord am thy Savior and thy Redeemer, the Mighty One of Jacob.

The answer to the question about will the lawful captive be delivered in God's judgment is a resounding – Yes! From a legalistic standpoint we would all be condemned, but in the Lord's system of judgment and grace, we are delivered. Because our Savior is the type of judge that delivers, rescues, saves, pleads for, advocates for, and redeems from oppressors, even those that are lawfully captive under the law can and will be delivered by Jesus Christ through His Atonement. For those suffering with scrupulosity this is resplendent good news! Too often the scrupulous worry about how they will be judged according to the laws of God from the perspective of a harsh, legalistic God seeking for ways to condemn them. Rather, we learn that God's judgement is more about saving, rescuing, delivering, and redeeming His "covenant people" from the law through Christ. In John 3:17 we learn:

17 For God sent not his Son into the world to condemn the world; but that the world through him might be saved.

In essence, God is looking for excuses to redeem us if we are willing to work with Him. He is trying to find a way to save us if we would just give Him a little bit of reason to do so. His orientation towards us is to bless us, not to condemn us. That should give the scrupulous great reason to hope. For we now know that we have our Best Friend in the Judgment Seat to judge us at the last day, and that His orientation towards us is to find ways to advocate on our behalf and seek to deliver us if we will just give Him any indication that we are willing to believe in Him, make and keep covenants with Him, and try to follow Him.

If you were on trial for some reason or another and had the opportunity to pick your absolute best friend who loves you, sees the good in you, has made tremendously unselfish sacrifices for you, and always has your back as the judge of your trial, wouldn't you jump at the chance to pick that sort of friend as your judge? That's the situation we find ourselves in with Christ. He is our Great Eternal Judge, but in that role He also is our Best Friend, our Advocate, our Redeemer, and our Savior. Additionally, because the Father and Son are "One" (meaning of one mind and purpose – see Doctrine and Covenants 50:43), we know that our Heavenly Father has the same orientation towards us as does Jesus, our Lord and Master.

This view of judgement reminds me of the statement by Pres. J. Reuben Clark, Jr. – a former counselor in the First Presidency who was also an amazing attorney for whom the BYU Law School is named – regarding the Lord's "juridical concept":

> "You know, I believe that the Lord will help us. I believe if we go to him, he will give us wisdom, if we are living righteously. I believe he will answer our prayers. I believe that our Heavenly Father wants to save every one of his children. I do not think he intends to shut any of us off because of some slight transgression, some slight failure to observe some rule or regulation. There are the great elementals that

we must observe, but he is not going to be captious about the lesser things.

"I believe that his juridical concept of his dealings with his children could be expressed in this way: I believe that in his justice and mercy, he will give us the maximum reward for our acts, give us all that he can give, and in the reverse, I believe that he will impose upon us the minimum penalty which it is possible for him to impose."[41]

Learning these concepts about judges and judgement really changed my approach to serving as a bishop. I didn't sit in my office and wait for those in need to come to me and beg for financial assistance or harshly condemn people punitively when they confessed their sins. Rather, I was actively out and about looking for opportunities to bless the lives of the saints in my ward both temporally and spiritually. I wanted them to come to know how readily God wanted to help and forgive them. I tried my best to help them understand how quick the Lord is to extend mercy, to deliver, to redeem, and to save. I learned that to judge is to save, not condemn. To judge is to advocate for and deliver relief and mercy to those in need, not to punish. I came to learn how quickly and eagerly God was and is to forgive the meekly penitent sinner even if their repentance is flawed or imperfect through no fault of their own, so long as they are honestly striving the best they can to sincerely repent. Their heart and a willing mind coupled with God's grace and power of redemption are sufficient for their most meager of efforts if they are given as their soul's whole offering (see Omni 1:26). God truly is a merciful God, and I have come to learn through both ecclesiastical and professional experiences that He is especially merciful to the scrupulous.

"GOD-ATTACHMENT" AND FAMILY OF ORIGIN WORK

Betty[1]* was a woman nearing retirement age. She came to see me for therapy in my private practice many years ago. She struggled with many mental health issues and diagnoses. She had been raised by austere parents who would always put her down. Whenever she would accomplish something and feel a sense of positive self-worth about it, her father, in particular, would say, "Well, don't get a big head about it." She felt she could never do anything right. She obsessed about whether or not God loved her. She always viewed Him as a harsh, punishing God the way her father was harsh and punishing to her. She struggled in her marriage, as well. One day she told me, "I don't know how to feel love for or from humans and I don't know how to feel love from God." I knew that Betty was a strong animal lover. She admitted that she did feel love from animals, especially her pets at home. In a moment of inspiration, I challenged her with this thought, "Don't you think that God is smart enough to know you'd have this problem, so since you don't feel His love directly from Him, He sends it to you indirectly through the animals. Their love for you is a reflection of His love for you." That changed everything for Betty. She began to understand that her mental health issues and history of parental put downs seemed to block her connection to

God, so He loved her so much to have a built-in work around so she'd still feel His love.

Betty's experience with her parents – her father in particular – is a common problem in the psycho-social-spiritual development of many people. Some people may project their experiences with their earthly parents (especially their father) onto God, our Heavenly Father.[2] They may have a hard time separating how their earthly father and mother have treated them from how Heavenly Father would treat them. They may assume God's orientation towards them is the same as they have experienced from their earthly parents.

Dr. Paul Vitz,[3] Professor Emeritus at New York University and a Senior Scholar at the Institute for the Psychological Sciences at Divine Mercy University, wrote an influential book called *Faith of the Fatherless: The Psychology of Atheism* which highlights the role parents – particularly fathers – play in shaping religious faith (and the lack of religious faith) of their children. By examining the father-child relationship patterns of historical figures – both prominent believers and atheists – he found a very strong correlation between poor, abusive, or absent father-child relationships and atheism. Dr. Vitz argues that the atheistic philosophies of Nietzsche, Freud, Sartre, Camus, and (to a lesser extent) Marx are discernable from patterns with their earthly fathers. Friedrich Nietzsche's father was a Protestant minister who died early in young Friedrich's childhood leaving a gaping emotional hole in his life. Nietzsche's famous statement, "God is dead"[4] is better psychologically understood as Nietzsche lamenting that his own earthly father is dead. Sartre, Camus, and others also suffered from dead or absent fathers, and this seems to be the source of impetus for their atheism. In the case of Sigmund Freud, Dr. Vitz points out that his father – Jacob Freud – was very weak and passive in the face of anti-Semitism, and that Sigmund Freud had hostility towards his father for being weak and lacking courage in anti-Semitic encounters. Jacob Freud spent long hours reading Jewish scripture and other writings with young Sigmund, so clearly Sigmund Freud associated religiosity with his father. But Jacob Freud had a deep, dark secret. In at least two of his personal letters, Sigmund Freud alludes to his father's sexual perversions and it is surmised that Sigmund's siblings (if not himself) were sexually abused by their father.[5] Sigmund Freud's rejection of and hostility towards religion is best understood as a negative, personal psychological projection he had about his father Jacob Freud onto God. The paternal pattern of Karl Marx is not so easily and clearly discernible. While there is no clear, obvious incident estranging Karl Marx from his father, Dr. Vitz cites the utter rejection of Karl Marx's father's values, financial status as a bourgeoisie, and religious devotion as "partial" evidence that Karl Marx's atheism may be linked to hostile feelings the younger Marx had for his father. Dr. Vitz's examination of at least twenty prominent historical atheists strongly supports his model for the "psychology of atheism" as springing from personal, poor experiences these philosophers had with their earthly fathers.

Conversely, Dr. Vitz uses over twenty historical figures illustrating how healthy relationships with their earthly fathers supported their faith in a Heavenly Father. Notable examples of father-child relationships of believers Dr. Vitz examined include: Blaise Pascal, Edmund Burke, Moses Mendelssohn, Alexis de Tocqueville, Soren Kierkegaard, Martin Buber, and Dietrich Bonhoeffer. In these cases, a strong correlation supports the thesis that healthy father-child relationships facilitated healthy relationships between those children and God.

So, what are we to make of this viewpoint that early childhood experiences with parents may shape whether or not we believe in God? How is this relevant for the scrupulous who already believe in God? I have a theory. I'll admit that this is an untested theory as of yet (more research would be needed to confirm this theory), but it is a theory that might hold some value (and has been helpful anecdotally with a few of my patients). I would posit the notion that not only do the early childhood experiences of parent-child relationships potentially shape whether or not we accept the *existence* of God, but that it might also color our perception about the *nature* of God. It is possible that our early parental encounters change our perception about the character, qualities, and attributes of God. Coming from a family

system characterized by harsh, exacting, rigid, and demanding parents might make projecting those characteristics onto God the next logical (though perhaps subconscious) step. As we have seen in the research literature, family perfectionism may be linked with scrupulosity.[6] Living in anxiety of the judgement and punishments of an earthly parent may lead the scrupulous to have similar anxieties about judgement from God.

It is necessary to see God for who He really is, not what we want Him to be or fear that He might be. Our faith proscribes that we come to know the "true God" (John 17:3), and that He is knowable through our experiencing of Him. Our Father in Heaven is a responsive, interactive God who yearns to engage and interrelate with us. In a scriptural sense, "knowing" someone is always an experiential, relational process rather than a cerebral, cognitive one.[7]

Often coming to know God in this experiential way is impeded by our personal history, trauma, and prior experiences with key people in our lives. Having a problem with parents and others in our family of origin can impede our ability to experience and know the true and living God. Dr. Tim Clinton and Dr. Joshua Straub address this very issue in their book *God Attachment: Why You Believe, Act, and Feel the Way You Do About God*.[8]

Clinton and Straub describe four styles of attachment: secure, anxious, avoidant, and fearful.[9] These attachment styles derive from our relationship patterns in early childhood with our parents or primary caregivers. When a parent is not perfect but "good enough" in giving consistent warm, safe, and caring responses to a child's needs, the child develops the idea that they are lovable and that relationships with people in general are safe and secure. Children with secure attachments to nurturing and caring parents grow up to feel comfortable with their emotions and can handle the joys and pitfalls of life more readily.

Children with anxious attachments typically have parents who are significantly inconsistent. Sometimes the parent responds to a child's needs with appropriate care, but at other times they respond with neglect, hostility, or indifference. The child never knows what to expect from such a parent so they become anxious when approaching the parent and ambivalent when the parent is responsive because they are waiting for the other shoe to drop and things to turn ugly.

Clinton and Straub[10] suggest that avoidant styles of attachment stem from parents who consistently neglect their child and see their child's pleas for support as "weakness or manipulation." Children from such parenting styles learn to take care of their own needs and be self-reliant but at the cost of valuing social connections and relationships. They learn to avoid relationships and assume relationships will only bring pain or disappointment. Relationships are anxiety provoking for the avoidant, but they tend to downplay their needs for relationships. In an "I can do it by myself" or "loner who doesn't need anyone else" manner, they go through life competing and clawing to get their own needs met and avoid emotional and relational connections.

Sometimes parents can be downright abusive and rear children in a chaotic, hostile environment. Children of such parents tend to learn to be fearful of others. Like the avoidant style, they socially stay away from emotions and intimate relationships, but unlike their avoidant counterparts they are not self-reliant and want self-worth and acceptance, but don't know how to get that need met. They tend to go through life very fearful and anxious.

Notice that in three of the four attachment styles (all but the secure attachment style) anxiety is the typical outcome. That anxiety may be manifest in myriad ways, but anxiety is a key underlying factor in their relationship styles. The scrupulous have anxiety about their relationships with God and others as a key characteristic. Their thoughts and behaviors – both with God and with their fellow men and women – are viewed through this anxious lens of self-examination and recrimination. In essence, they project this harsh attachment style learned in childhood onto God's judgment of themselves.

Perhaps, this is one way to understand Paul's counsel to "put away childish things" and cease seeing "through a glass, darkly" (1 Cor. 13:11-12). If we stop viewing God through the dark glass or dim lens of our early parent-child attachment style relationships and come to know Him for who He really is, we can cast off the "God-attachment" style of our childhood and come to know Him in a more safe, secure way. For the scrupulous this task of healing their "God-attachment" and coming to know Him as loving and merciful rather than harsh and legalistically judgmental is essential.

One individual I worked with around his scrupulosity was Craig.[11*] Craig was a member of the Church in his early thirties who got headaches every time he did something he feared might be a sin until he confessed to his bishop. This psychosomatic response was a unique consequence of his scrupulous OCD. He was a single man and had lots of concerns about appropriate dating behavior, such as "Is passionate kissing a sin?" as well as other concerns about what is appropriate sabbath behavior, such as "Is watching a sitcom on Sunday afternoon okay?" He would obsess over these kinds of questions and get a headache until he was able to "confess" to his bishop and get relief. As we counseled together and reviewed the Foundational Truths in the first stage of my treatment approach, he struggled with seeing God in a merciful way. I asked him about his attachment patterns to his family of origin. He said he had a decent relationship with his mother and siblings but his relationship with his father was problematic. When I inquired further about his relationship with his father he told me, "I've never had a meaningful conversation with my dad in my life." He described his father as socially inept (he speculated that his father might be autistic). His father went to work in a field where he didn't have to work with people – just numbers. His father would come home and basically ignore the family by watching a lot of TV. If his father spoke to him at all it was either to order him around (things like, "Go get me a soda") or to yell and punish him. As we further processed his issues with his father, Craig began to see how he had developed a harsh, distant, and punitive view of Heavenly Father because of his earthly father's treatment of him. I worked with Craig urging him to separate the punitive earthly father from his loving Heavenly Father, helping him come to clearly know God for who He really is un-hindered from the dark, harsh, and terrifying lens his earthly father provided.

In some ways, it is as if scrupulous people are trying to see God as He really is, but they are wearing distorted sunglasses. The distorted sunglasses are their experiences with their earthly parents. By doing family of origin work and exploring their childhood attachment styles, they can remove the sunglasses and begin to see God clearly. When they do so, they find Him far more loving and merciful than they ever could have imagined. Their "God-attachment" style can change to a secure relationship even if their parent-child attachment style was something quite different.

Another person who I did therapy with for her scrupulosity was Hannah.[12*] I was trying to help her see God in a less judgmental way, but she was struggling to accept the ideas I was discussing with her about a merciful, loving Father who encourages us in our growth and development. I decided to try guided imagery with her to get a better idea of how she saw God's role in judging her. I asked her to close her eyes and imagine it was the Day of Judgment. I tried to get her to describe what she thought she would see and experience on that future day. She tried but got a little frustrated. Finally, she opened her eyes and said to me, "Honestly, what I saw was Jesus and my dad laughing at me." In follow-up questions it became evident that they were "laughing" at her in the form of ridicule because of all her mistakes and failures. I asked her about her relationship with her dad (her earthly father). She defensively pointed out what a good father he was and how he provided for her. She even pointed out that he was a prominent priesthood leader in the Church. I reassured her that I wasn't looking to place blame on her parents. Most parents do their best to love and support their children, but sometimes even the best of us struggle in some dimensions of family relationships. She then began to describe how her father was emotionally distant from her in some ways and was very fastidious about Gospel standards. In their home they were only allowed to listen to Gospel-oriented music (no secular music was ever allowed in the home) and were expected to stringently live the Gospel in an assiduous way. When I asked about her mother, Hannah said she, too, was emotionally distant and demanding. Upon reflection, she saw a connection between how her family perfectionistic upbringing in her home contributed to her scrupulous view of God as exacting, demanding, and stringent about even the most minute details of Gospel living. I encouraged her to separate some of those more stringent experiences with her earthly parents from how she viewed her Heavenly Father and the Savior. This helped her begin to ease her scrupulosity and have a healthier relationship with God.

For many generations now, the cultural assumption in the Church was that members come from "goodly parents" and that parental teaching will imbue future generations with a legacy of strength. Church leaders have sought to establish gospel-centered "multigenerational families" of strong spiritual strength. That is a lofty and commendable goal we should strive to obtain, but we must recognize many members of the Church just aren't there yet. Not all members of the Church have loving, Gospel-oriented families where good parenting promotes both spiritual and mental health. Building multigenerationally strong, gospel-centered families takes just that – generations. As a Church with increasing numbers of converts (and as Satan's attack on the family advances and leads to increased family dysfunction broadly) many members of the Church simply did not have "goodly parents" who set an example of Gospel living. Perhaps, my experience as a therapist has brought me into contact with so many who suffer from poor parenting that I am predisposed to see the challenges all families face, but we simply cannot assume strong parenting (without accompanying personal, individual effort) will be sufficient to help avoid false and hurtful perceptions of God in the rising generations. And even in the case where there have been "goodly parents," we can't rely solely on heritage for our individual personal spirituality. Flawed perspectives on God that over-emphasize harshness and rigidity may still perpetuate themselves. Each person must come to know God independently and experience Him as He truly is for themselves. We must have our own personal revelation to come to know the correct character and nature of our loving Heavenly Father and be guided through personal revelation as counseled by President Russell M. Nelson:

"If we are to have any hope of sifting through the myriad of voices and the philosophies of men that attack truth, we must learn to receive revelation.

"Our Savior and Redeemer, Jesus Christ, will perform some of His mightiest works between now and when He comes again. We will see miraculous indications that God the Father and His Son, Jesus Christ, preside over this Church in majesty and glory. But in coming days, it will not be possible to survive spiritually without the guiding, directing, comforting, and constant influence of the Holy Ghost."[13]

Please don't misunderstand me. Parents absolutely play a vital role in helping children grow up knowing God. The new balance of a "home-centered, Church-supported" perspective on the Gospel underscores the role of parents in teaching in the home, but parental influence must be coupled with the youth's own personal religious behaviors.[14] Too often, parents' own unresolved spiritual problems get passed down to their children. Coming to know God for who He really is, without the spiritual "baggage" of the traditions of forefathers, is a very freeing experience in our own spiritual maturation process. For all members of the Church, we must come to learn how truly perfect God is in every way – kind, just, merciful, loving, omniscient, and wise. The experience of getting to know God through revelation, scripture, service, and the witness of the Holy Ghost is a greater developer of spirituality than any other mechanism.

I've come to learn that Patriarchal Blessings are one of the most sublime ways we can come to know the true God and our true selves within the context of our sacred covenant relationship with Him. These Patriarchal Blessings are a personal window into our souls and help us to see ourselves through God's perspective. In the process we also come to see God more clearly. Indeed, there is great truth in Joseph Smith's statement, "If men do not comprehend the character of God, they do not comprehend themselves."[15] When my wife, as a convert to the Church at age 22, received her Patriarchal Blessing, the patriarch stated that Heavenly Father had looked forward to this day to "reveal to her who she really was" and proceeded to instruct her as His daughter about her talents, gifts, and responsibilities in life. I've come to learn that Patriarchal blessings often serve the purpose of revealing to us who we really are in the sight of God, and that such a sacred window into our soul is opened as we receive His perspective of us into our hearts and minds. As we do so, we will "grow, develop, and progress" into the fulfilment of His purposes for our creation.

Once again, understanding the "Gospel of Growth" perspective is relevant here. The Gospel is our Father's mechanism to facilitate our spiritual growth and progression. Just as human development follows natural stages of progression, spiritual development of faith also follows predictable stages. Dr. James Fowler's[16] book *Stages of Faith* is a classic text in understanding how spiritual development parallels patterns of human development outlined by Piaget, Erikson, Kohlberg, and other notable scholars in the field of child and human development.

Fowler posits six stages of faith that correlate to a degree with stages of human development. There is a pre-stage that infants have which he calls "Undifferentiated Faith." Then his six stages are: 1. Intuitive-Projective (Early Childhood), 2. Mythic-Literal Faith (School Years), 3. Synthetic-Conventional Faith (Adolescence), 4. Individuative-Reflective Faith (Young Adulthood), 5. Conjunctive Faith (Mid-Life and Beyond), and 6. Universalizing Faith (Rare).

Is it possible that Fowler's "stages of faith" can give us some insight into scrupulosity? I don't know for certain, but I believe so. I do not have confirmed research supporting this conclusion. It is just a theory, but it is a theory informed by anecdotal experiences with patients and a comment by one scholar who noted that "religious devotion can influence the focus and experience of obsessive-compulsive symptoms.[17] Let me be clear that I am not stating that a person with scrupulosity needs to have more faith or needs to try harder to develop their faith in a way that would suddenly ease their obsessional concerns. That is just not the case. What I am suggesting is that family of origin experiences that include training a child that God is a harsh, punitive Being *might* lead to an "overestimation of threat" maladaptive belief – that it might lead to children overestimating God as a threat. As one of the six key maladaptive beliefs that fuels OCD, any family of origin experiences (including how children are taught about God) that might lead to a person's overestimation of the threat of God might be a significant influence in the expression of their OCD as scrupulosity.

I am well aware that OCD has biological and genetic causes[18] (and possibly even a combination of environmental and biological factors like exposure to certain infections that have been linked to OCD), so I am not theorizing that faith development has a causal link to OCD. That simply wouldn't be true. But I do wonder if the *expression* of that OCD in religious terms (as opposed to contamination/hand-washing, hoarding, symmetry, counting, checking, and so forth) might have anything to do with cognitive processes (for example, the formation of maladaptive beliefs) formed through family of origin experiences in a person's human development as they progress through the stages of faith development? In other words, I believe that the individual with scrupulosity would have developed OCD regardless of the faith development trajectory in their childhood. But, there is a lack of consensus among scholars about what causes the subtypes of OCD (or if the subtypes themselves are the appropriate discreet categories).[19] We do see that OCD tends to "attack" the things people value the most, but we are unsure as to why that is. In the absence of research confidence about the causes of subtypes, could it be that family of origin experiences around rigid and punitive religious upbringing may be a possible contributory factor to the development of the subtype of OCD as scrupulosity (as opposed to other subtypes such as contamination concerns, counting, checking, etc.)? Might family of origin experiences that teach that God is a harsh, punitive Being (and any other faith development experiences that were overly rigid, punitive, and legalistic) lead to the cognitive and affective formation of the six maladaptive beliefs that fuel OCD (inflated responsibility, overestimated threat, importance of thought, control of thoughts, perfectionism, and intolerance of uncertainty)? We simply do not know. It is a possible theory, but not a certain one. Yet, if we ask ourselves in what stage of human and spiritual development would parental emphasis on religious rigidity and the harshness of God lead to anxiety and OCD being manifested in scrupulous terms rather than other subtypes of OCD, I believe Fowler's "stages of faith" model might have some answers, particularly in the context of attachment theory and human development regarding family of origin influences.

From infancy, babies are poised to attach and learn to trust their parents or other caregivers. They have an "undifferentiated faith" because their faith or trust in their parents (depending on the consistency of nurture and care they receive) is not differentiated from their faith in God. Essentially, the attachment processes established in infancy are the building blocks for future stages of faith. Fowler describes this process in his chapter on "Undifferentiated Faith":

> "In the pre-stage called Undifferentiated faith, the seeds of trust, courage, hope and love are fused in an undifferentiated way and contend with sensed threats of abandonment, inconsistencies and deprivations in an infant's environment. ...(T)he quality of mutuality and strength of trust, autonomy, hope and courage (or their opposites) developed in this phase underlie (or threaten to undermine) all that comes later in faith development."[20]

Thus, we see that early infancy parent-child interactions may have later implications for the child's faith development trajectory. Specifically, insecure or harsh parent-child interactions may lead to "overestimation of threat" cognitive belief processes.

Fowler's first stage – Intuitive-Projective faith – is found in children ages two to six or seven years old. Using their "new tools of speech and symbolic representation" to make meaning of the world, children at this stage use imagination to construct their simple views of God. They project their faith from the stories they are taught at Church and in the home onto God and base their experiences with God largely on how their parents' teachings and examples frame the child's experiences. This is why parental teaching is so vital to how children develop their faith in God. The parents set the early parameters and most children do not question or develop different views of God until further stages of development. Fowler warns that at this stage of faith development that the "...imagination and fantasy life of the child can be exploited by witting or unwitting adults."[21] He goes on at length to provide a contrast between parents who provide spiritual stories that help the child to feel safe and secure in their faith in God from those who emphasize fear, rigidity, and the harshness of God's punishments:

> "For every child whose significant others have shared religious stories, images and symbols in ways that prove life-opening and sustaining of love, faith and courage, there must be at least one other for whom the introduction to religion, while equally powerful, gave rise to fear, rigidity, and the brutalization of souls – both one's own and those of others. There are religious groups who subject Intuitive-Projective children to the kind of preaching and teaching that vividly emphasize the pervasiveness and power of the devil, the sinfulness of all people without Christ and the hell of fiery torments that await the unrepentant. That kind of faith formation – and its equivalent in other religious traditions – can ensure a dramatic 'conversion experience' by the time the child is seven or eight. It runs grave risk, however, of leading to... 'precocious identity formation' in which the child, at conversion, takes on the adult faith identity called for by the religious group. This often results when a child is an adult in the emergence of a very rigid, brittle, and authoritarian personality."[22]

This developmental trajectory can be a possible precursor to a person seeing God as a threat. From these early stages children who will eventually struggle with OCD may experience religion in a way that exacerbates that OCD into the form called scrupulosity. Children for whom religion conveys "fear, rigidity, and the brutalization of souls" may experience God as a "very rigid, brittle, and authoritarian personality" matching the religious experience of their early childhood. In this way, family of origin experiences and early childhood religious teachings of parents and others may contribute to existing risk factors (i.e. OCD's genetic, biological, and environmental predispositions) for the development of scrupulosity.

While the OCD will likely still come in a person's life due to their predispositions, it may be possible to avoid it taking the form of scrupulosity if the religious training of a child's life emphasizes the loving, merciful, and gracious nature of God. Fowler specifically emphasizes that healthy spiritual training comes from emphasizing parables and stories with children.[23] Parents, primary teachers, and others should emphasize parables and stories that show God's love and mercy to young children. Elder Neil L. Andersen's April 2010 General Conference talk, "Tell Me the Stories of Jesus,"[24] is an excellent example of how to teach young children from scripture stories and parables about the Savior and His loving kindness and compassionate nature.

Fowler's second stage is the Mythic-Literal faith. At around age eight years old (interestingly the age of accountability in our faith), Piaget's developmental model suggests that children move into concrete-operational thinking. This is when children understand how the world works in concrete terms. They separate what is real from what is make believe. They focus on rules and what is right and what is wrong according to the rules. This is why children at this age love games (whether sports, board games, or other structured play) where rules are important, and may insist (even argue) over the smallest detail or rule. According to Fowler, it is in this stage that children develop a concrete understanding of who God is and what He looks like. He gives examples from interviews with children and concludes:

> "The anthropomorphic elements in [the child's] image of God (the old man with the white beard who lives on top of the world) as in many of our stage 2 interviews, are far more developed than the nascent anthropomorphic images in [another child's] depiction of God quoted in our discussion of stage 1."[25]

We are blessed as Latter-day Saints to know from the First Vision and other theophanies of the Restoration what God looks like and that He is a Man with flesh and bones and that we are literally created in His image.[26] But it is important to note that at this age children form a sense of the nature, attributes, and character of God, as well as His physical features. As we've discussed previously, it is vital to have a *correct* understanding of the nature, attributes, and character of God to alleviate symptoms of scrupulosity.

Fowler also suggests one other key fact pertaining to Stage 2 that may relate to scrupulosity. Fowler suggests that in this stage children develop a "similar understanding of reciprocal justice as an immanent structure in our lives. Presumably God created this ordering of things and even God is bound to the lawfulness he has created."[27] Of course it is true that God follows the Laws of Heaven. He cannot rob justice for mercy's sake.[28] He is a God of truth and cannot lie.[29] If He were to do so, He would cease to be God (and that will never happen). But that doesn't mean He is mean and ruthless in the process of following His own laws. Instead, He created a plan whereby justice *and* mercy can coexist and synergistically inform one another. As mentioned earlier, Pres. J. Reuben Clark stated:

> "You know, I believe that the Lord will help us. I believe if we go to him, he will give us wisdom, if we are living righteously. I believe he will answer our prayers. I believe that our Heavenly Father wants to save every one of his children. I do not think he intends to shut any of us off because of some slight transgression, some slight failure to observe some rule or regulation. There are the great elementals that we must observe, but he is not going to be captious about the lesser things.
>
> "I believe that his juridical concept of his dealings with his children could be expressed in this way: I believe that in his justice and mercy, he will give us the maximum reward for our acts, give us all that he can give, and in the reverse, I believe that he will impose upon us the minimum penalty which it is possible for him to impose."[30]

Heavenly Father sent His Son to meet the demands of justice

through His Atonement so that mercy can be extended to all of Heavenly Father's children. On one level, mercy is universally applied in that all who have been born and received a body will be resurrected. What a merciful act to ensure the sting of death is not forever! We are all blessed with the promise that death is merely a short part of our eternal existence. Additionally, mercy is extended to any who will meet the "conditions of repentance"[31] and follow the laws and ordinances of the Gospel through the Atonement of Jesus Christ. But this idea of what really and fully constitutes the "conditions of repentance" and did the scrupulously penitent person really follow the laws and ordinances of the Gospel with exactness is often at the heart of the obsessional haunting of the scrupulous. What Fowler describes as the laws of "reciprocal justice" might be likened to what Latter-day Saints call God's "conditions of repentance" and an over-anxious concern to the extreme on this way of thinking may contribute to the scrupulosity of the sufferer. This stage emphasizes laws and lawfulness. It is seeking to know God obliquely according to His rules and laws rather than knowing Him personally through interacting with Him as He really is. It is a cognitive knowledge of God rather than an experiential-relational way of knowing God. As the person seeks to know God through legalism at this stage, they are susceptible to maladaptive beliefs about inflated responsibility, overestimation of threat, importance of thought, control of thoughts, perfectionism, and intolerance of uncertainty. Rigid and harsh religious rearing at this stage might be a risk factor for the maladaptive beliefs that fuel OCD.

Fowler describes the extreme version of Stage 2 Mythic-Literal thinking in terms that sound a lot like the OCD of the scrupulous:

> "The limitations of literalness and excessive reliance on reciprocity as a principle for constructing an ultimate environment can result in either an overcontrolling, stilted perfectionism or 'works righteousness' or in their opposite, an abasing sense of badness embraced because of mistreatment, neglect or the apparent disfavor of significant others."[32]

Such a description of scrupulosity could not be more apt – "over-controlling, stilted perfectionism" and placing faith in what other Christian faiths call "works righteousness" (or what Allen and his colleagues define as legalism, which they found to be a potentially predictive factor of scrupulosity)[33] whereby we believe we can live in exact obedience to God's laws and "earn" our way into heaven (and when that fails we start "abasing" ourselves and feel bad or unworthy) rather than relying on the mercy of Christ and His atoning grace.

I believe the Lord wants His people to live in a "higher and holier way"[34] by compassionately ministering to one another and applying those same principles in a self-compassionate way. Those suffering with scrupulosity must place this harsh, distorted view of God's judgment on the altar of sacrifice to be let go of and begin to embrace through faith the mercy of God's grace and compassion as His preferred style of justice and judgment whereby judgment is defined as redeeming, delivering, and rescuing the oppressed from their mental health concerns.

Let me give you a personal example, I was recently asked to give an elderly dying woman a blessing before she departed this life. Though not a member of our faith, she had relatives who were active in our Church and she had been acquainted with the Gospel in life. I happened to know that this woman had experienced a hard life and struggled with many things such as addiction and abusiveness which caused much suffering to her family members. Nevertheless, they loved her despite her failings. As I pronounced a blessing I was surprised that I was inspired by the Holy Ghost to bless her to know that Heavenly Father was pleased with her life "given the context of her circumstances." From my mortal perspective, it would have been too easy to judge this woman by her failures, but God knew her life's circumstances and the mitigating factors. He considered these factors in His judgment of her and taught me that I was not aware of these mitigating factors and should defer my flawed, mortal judgments to His wisdom. Though His sense of justice may not fit our mortal senses of judgment, His ways are higher than our ways. In Isaiah 55: 8-9 we read:

8 For my thoughts are not your thoughts, neither are your ways my ways, saith the Lord.

9 For as the heavens are higher than the earth, so are my ways higher than your ways, and my thoughts than your thoughts.

As I pondered upon this experience, I thought how often I had judged people without the full knowledge that God has about them. In some of the instances (for example when I was a bishop), the Lord would reveal things to me that were "mitigating factors" and I could see how a more merciful approach (compared to my more mortal judgments of them) was actually the more just approach. So, to the suffering scrupulous who cannot seem to fathom how God could do anything but condemn them, I would offer that God knows the mitigating factors of our lives better than we know even of ourselves. Therefore, we must learn to bend to His will and trust in His mercy when He extends it to us rather than insist on a form of justice that bends His will to the distorted justice of our mortal minds. In all of my experiences working with the penitent as a Church leader and as a therapist working with mental health issues, I have been constantly amazed at how merciful, loving, and forgiving God is. That doesn't mean people get a free pass to sin. Sadly, I've sat in councils where the unrepentant have had to face disciplinary measures that set boundaries and meted out consequences according to the justice of God. Many had hardened their hearts and proclaimed they no longer believed in God and/or the Church – what I term the "I sin, therefore I disbelieve" philosophy. Those councils with the impenitent are sad experiences, indeed. But, in contrast, where a soul shows true remorse and a willingness to repent, mercy seems to rule over the proceedings. In all my years serving in various disciplinary councils of the Church, I've never been in a situation where the Lord hasn't made His will known *abundantly* clear with a vast outpouring of the Spirit to his presiding authorities of such councils. It is as if the issue of the penitent's standing before God is of such sacred importance that the Lord wants absolutely no mistake to be made, and so He abundantly reveals

His will to the judge of Israel in the matter. So, when a person with scrupulosity receives counsel from a judge of Israel telling them the matter has been resolved before the Lord, the scrupulous sufferer can rely upon that with full confidence, even if they struggle to forgive themselves and still feel to condemn themselves.

Elder Richard G. Scott once spoke clearly on this matter:

"Now if you are one who cannot forgive yourself for serious past transgressions—even when a judge in Israel has assured that you have properly repented—if you feel compelled to continually condemn yourself and suffer by frequently recalling the details of past errors, I plead with all of my soul that you ponder this statement of the Savior:

"He who has repented of his sins, the same is forgiven, and I, the Lord, remember them no more.

"By this ye may know if a man repenteth of his sins— ... he will confess them and forsake them."

"To continue to suffer when there has been proper repentance is not prompted by the Savior but the master of deceit, whose goal is to bind and enslave you. Satan will press you to continue to relive the details of past mistakes, knowing that such thoughts make forgiveness seem unattainable. In this way Satan attempts to tie strings to the mind and body so that he can manipulate you like a puppet.

"I testify that when a bishop or stake president has confirmed that your repentance is sufficient, know that your obedience has allowed the Atonement of Jesus Christ to satisfy the demands of justice for the laws you have broken. Therefore, you are now free. Please believe it. To continually suffer the distressing effects of sin after adequate repentance, while not intended, is to deny the efficacy of the Savior's Atonement in your behalf."[35]

More comforting words were never more appropriately applied than this tender counsel from Elder Scott to the scrupulous.

In Fowler's third stage – Synthetic-Conventional – the development of faith coincides with an adolescent's development of their identity. It focuses on knowing God and knowing one's self in relation to God. At the core of this type of faith, Fowler describes, an "adolescent's religious hunger is for a God who knows, accepts and confirms the self deeply, and who serves as an infinite guarantor of the self with its forming myth of personal identity and faith."[36] By "myth" Fowler means the teen's developing story or narrative that they are constructing about themselves and is at the heart of their sense of personal worth.

We all form a sense of self based on the experiences we have with others. As a child, parents serve as a "looking-glass" or mirror from which the child sees themselves based on the parents' comments and attitudes they give to the child. For example, if a little girl is singing in the living room and the child's mother says, "Oh Sally, I love to hear your pretty voice," the mother is observing the child's behavior, evaluating or judging it, and then reflecting it back to the child so the child can use the information to construct a sense of her little self. Now, based on her mother's evaluative comment, Sally believes she has a pretty singing voice. Over hundreds and thousands of similar experiences – some good, some hurtful – children develop an emerging sense of self. But in the adolescent years, their interactions (and the valuations of those interactions) extend beyond family and early school peers to many, many more people. The teen must synthesize the information from these broader sources to construct a coherent sense of self called an "identity." The problem with all of these interactions is that the "others" (parents, friends, teachers, and so forth) have their own personal distortions and biases. They are not a perfect mirror. Like the funhouse with convex and concave mirrors that distort our images, the distorted "others" in a teen's life help them construct their own distorted approximation of who they are, but not necessarily an accurate one. Because self-worth still involves the distorted flaw of self-perception based on the input from others, people must be careful in relying too heavily on the self-identity they tend to construct based on mortal perceptions of those around us. In one sense, only God is the "Perfect Mirror" whose perception of us is undistorted. As we are willing to shed our distorted self-perceived images and come to see us as how God sees us, we can transcend this synthetic-conventional approach and develop a more mature faith (and healthier identity). For the scrupulous, having a distorted sense of self (usually low self-worth) and a distorted sense of God (usually harsh and legalistic) based on their earlier childhood and family of origin experiences might make this stage of faith development extremely difficult. Those that get stuck in synthesizing their spiritual identity from these distorted sources and never truly coming to know God and themselves for who He (and they) really are – coupled with other predispositions toward OCD – might be at risk for scrupulosity. Working out a healthy sense of self-worth based on God's perspective and coming to know the true worth of their soul in the sight of God is crucial for all people spiritually. But it is even more essential for those with OCD/scrupulosity so that they can eliminate false distortions whereby their brain becomes "locked" or stuck and be able to address their mental health concerns free of the concomitant spiritual fears they have.

Fowler warns that some may become stuck in this stage of development due to the "expectations and evaluations of others" becoming "internalized (and sacralized)" and that a person's capacity for individual, autonomous "judgment and action can be jeopardized."[37] Once again, that sounds like an apt description of the "evaluative concerns" dimension of maladaptive perfectionism that scholars have linked with scrupulosity.[38] Impairment of judgment and action because the sufferer has internalized and sacralized distorted views of God and others are clinical features of this mental illness.

Fowler's fourth stage is called the Individuative-Reflective stage. Typically, as young single adults leave home to go to college, work, or serve in the military, they are extracted from the external authority of the parents and home they grew up in. They will go through a period of questioning and seeking their own answers to life's ultimate questions. Typically, it is a time where the emerging adult questions external authority. For Latter-day Saints, there is a similar process

(though not all will necessarily question all external authorities such as God, the Prophet, or the Brethren), but even most LDS young adults do wrestle with serious questions about what they individually and personally believe as opposed to what they have been taught to believe by their parents and family members. In LDS parlance we may say this is a period where they can "no longer live on borrowed light." They have to come to know the truth of the Gospel and develop an emerging deep faith on their own for themselves (if they have not done so in previous stages of development). Service as a missionary is the quintessential learning and growing experience whereby an emerging adult comes to embrace faith and garner a strong testimony on his or her own. It is a time when they can more fully experience and interact with Him in their daily work. Faith in God, the Savior's Atonement, and the Restoration of the Gospel becomes their own and not something based on external authority. They experience God for themselves and come to know Him in their extremities and encounters of life. Fowler states that the "relocation of authority within the self" and extraction or distancing from one's previous social and familial milieu which leads to the "emergence of an executive ego" are critical steps to developing this more mature form of faith.[39] Perhaps, this may account for some Latter-day Saints developing adaptive perfection based on personal strivings vs. maladaptive perfectionism based on evaluative concerns of others. In this more mature, self-driven faith the person must "take seriously the burden of responsibility for his or her own commitments, lifestyle, belief, and attitudes" and must grapple with "unavoidable tensions" within their faith and the realities of the world they live in whereby a new sense of "identity (self) and outlook (ideology)" move from just going along with what they've been taught to what they really think and feel about God and the world around them.[40]

I believe that for the scrupulous, they struggle with seeing themselves as a competent expert on spiritual matters in their life. One scholar also mentions this as an issue for the scrupulous. Clark suggests that the scrupulous have a "negative self-perception (that) might contribute to a propensity to misinterpret the significance of unwanted intrusive thoughts perceived as relevant to the individual's self-construct" and that "individuals with OCD have a fragile or ambivalent self-view that contributes to a greater likelihood that unwanted ego-dystonic intrusions will be misinterpreted as meaningful threats to valued aspects of self.[41] This leads to self-recrimination and anxious control of thoughts processes. They keep striving to have an "external authority" (a parent, a friend, a bishop, or other Church leader) evaluate their concerns and decide their spiritual standing because they don't have confidence in themselves. They don't trust their own individual reflections on spiritual matters and seek to rely on the external authority of others' opinions.

I would be very surprised to see someone still suffering with scrupulosity able to engage in Fowler's fifth and sixth stages meaningfully unless they have done a lot of healing work through therapy, soul-searching growth, and significant pastoral counseling. It is a kind of faith most people, in general, don't achieve, let alone those who struggle with scrupulosity. I don't believe stages five (Conjunctive Faith) and six (Universalizing Faith) would contribute to or worsen any sufferer with scrupulosity, but there may be some answers or solutions in these last two stages of Fowler's model that could benefit those struggling with scrupulosity.

Conjunctive Faith (stage five) is hard to parsimoniously describe. It involves several facets. Fowler calls it "faith-knowing" which seems a lot like the certainty that some Latter-day Saints would describe when saying their faith has moved from mere deeply-held, personal belief to a knowledge gained through revelation and other witnesses of the Spirit. That seems to be part of it, but there's also more to it. Fowler describes this type of knowing as:

> "a way of seeing, of knowing, of committing, [that] moves beyond the dichotomizing logic of Stage 4's 'either/or.' It sees both (or the many) sides of an issue simultaneously. Conjunctive faith suspects that things are organically related to each other; it attends to the pattern of interrelatedness in things, trying to avoid force-fitting to its own prior mindset.

"The phrase 'dialectical knowing' comes close to describing Stage 5's style, yet the term is too methodologically controlling. Better, I think, to speak of *dialogical* knowing. In dialogical knowing the known is invited to speak in its own word in its own language. In dialogical knowing the multiplex structure of the world is invited to disclose itself. In a mutual 'speaking' and 'hearing,' knower and known converse in an I-Thou relationship...

"Stage 5's willingness... is not merely a function of the knower's self-certainty. It also has to do with the trustworthiness of the known. In this sense Stage 5 represents a kind of complementarity or mutuality in relation."[42]

Some examples Fowler gives to describe this type of knowing in Stage 5 is:

"Realizing that the behavior of light requires that it be understood both as a wave phenomenon *and* as particles of energy...

"Looking at a field of flowers simultaneously through a microscope and a wide-angle lens."[43]

CONJUNCTIVE FAITH SEEMS to be able to make sense of the paradoxes of life. Perhaps, this would help the scrupulous saint better navigate the paradoxes of OCD treatment and healing that we will discuss in subsequent chapters. Through Conjunctive Faith we can see many sides or facets and find a way to put them together as part of a whole. This is what marriage and family therapists often do in our work through what we call "Systems Theory." We are able to see all sides and see how they can be joined or coincide with the bigger picture of the system as a whole. Fowler is suggesting that Conjunctive Faith is a type of knowing whereby the truth speaks for itself and that the truth has many facets and can be understood from many perspectives. That allows for the complexity and the simplicity of truth to both be accurate. What is known (or true) simply exists independent of what it does for the person knowing. In other words, it isn't something that the person of faith can create to meet their own needs (like the identity needs of previous stages), but that doesn't mean the knower of the known is irrelevant. The "interrelatedness" of the knower and the known benefits the knower because he or she can take himself or herself out of it and just view the truth from differing points of view.

This is essential for the scrupulous – to learn to take their own obsessions and compulsions out of the equation, so to speak, and simply let the truth of matters speak for themselves. It is also painfully difficult for them to do because allowing the truth to speak for itself is full of anxiety-provoking possibilities. But learning to take out all of the angles, arguments, rationalizations, and guessing (and second-guessing) from multiple perspectives that comprise the mental anguish of the "doubting disease" of scrupulosity can be healing. Learning to submit to and accept the truth that God loves them and wants to grow them rather than condemn them can be freeing and relieving. Learning to not listen to all the "noise" of obsessions, anxieties, fears, and doubts – that God will not speak to them through doubt and fear but only through clear, unmistakable ways that bolster faith and lead to light helps them separate the inspirational information from the naysaying noise of negativity. This does not mean that the scrupulous are incapable of sin and never need to repent. Of course, they do need to repent, as do we all! But I have come to learn that when a person with scrupulosity truly commits a sin, God will invite them to repent in clear, unmistakable ways that leave no doubt at all about what they have to do to repent. He does not speak in the shadows of half-truth, half-doubt, nor flip-flopping through the murky heights and depths of insecurity and anxiety. No, He is too merciful to do that to the scrupulous. If they are experiencing such sallying back and forth in their minds, they can be assured this is part of the mental illness of scrupulosity.

This stage allows the scrupulous sufferer to be humble and open to learning from God as they rid themselves of the opinions of others and even themselves. As the scrupulous get out of their own way and learn to listen to God and not themselves, they can come to the truth of things "as they are, and as they were, and as they are to come." (Doctrine and Covenants 93:24) even if such truths seem paradoxical to what they already know. They will come to understand that things that may not make sense from their own limited perspective might look very different from God's perspective, for He sees the "multiplex" structure of all things – including their systemic, interrelatedness – from the perspective of omniscience and we do not. Therefore, learning to accept His mercy, grace, and forgiveness – even when it may not make sense to us – is an act of humbly accepting His knowledge and wisdom are higher than our own.

Fowler's sixth and final stage is called Universalizing Faith and he states it is "exceedingly rare."[44] He suggests that the person who transitions to Stage 6 becomes a "moral and ascetic actualization of the universalizing" truths, and that they are heedless of the "threats to self, to primary groups, and to the institutional arrangements of the present order."[45] Fowler goes on to describe a person with Universalizing Faith as one who "becomes a disciplined, activist *incarnation* – a making real and tangible – of the imperatives of absolute love and justice" and who "engages in spending and being spent for the transformation of present reality in the direction of a transcendent actuality." Persons in history who would qualify as achieving Universalizing Faith, according to Fowler, would be people like Gandhi, Martin Luther King, Jr., Mother Teresa of Calcutta, Dag Hammarskjold, Dietrich Bonhoeffer, Abraham Heschel, and Thomas Merton.

The ultimate incarnation of love, truth, justice, and mercy – the most universalizing faith ever known among all of God's children – is found in our Savior, Jesus Christ, according to Latter-day Saint beliefs. He is ever the Exemplar we should all look to, but it is helpful to see others who, during their mortal sojourn in life, gave all so unselfishly for the benefit of all humanity. He disrupted the social order of His day and refused to follow the rules and false traditions of the Pharisees and Sadducees because those rules were myopic misapplications of the doctrines, principles, and laws that He, as the Great Lawgiver, had universally given centuries earlier.[46] In my estimation, Joseph Smith, Jr. and many of the prophets – both ancient and modern – to one degree or another approximated this universal love for all of God's children and the desire to see Christ's teachings not only taught, but lived as He did.

In regards to scrupulosity, the key lesson they can learn from Universalizing Faith is to emphasize "being" rather than doing. None of us will ever "be" as Jesus lived during mortal life, but we can strive to focus on "being" with people, loving people, loving God, loving ourselves, being holy, and ministering to people as Jesus would. If the scrupulous can get away from a "checklist of perfectionism" mentality or a behavioral focus on "was that a sin, and if so what do I have to *do* to repent?" towards living as a way of *being-as-godly-as-can-be* mentality, they will have learned something of universalizing faith that may heal them to a degree. By focusing on growing and developing, rather than performing a checklist of do's and don'ts before a wrathful, harsh, and legalistic God, the scrupulous can cultivate their lives like a beautiful garden of love that is watched over and cared for by a loving, merciful God.

Elder Bruce C. Hafen once taught, "We need grace both to overcome sinful weeds and to grow divine flowers. We can do neither one fully by ourselves."[47] God is in the business of growing us into godhood. He wants His children to grow to the full measure of their creation so that they can find the joy and happiness that He has. A God who wants to share His lifestyle with His children doesn't seem to me to be one who is looking for chances to punish us. He expects us to work hard to grow by eliminating unholy things from our lives and character and embrace faith and holiness. He sent the Savior to provide grace, repentance, and healing to overcome all things – even mental illness – that prevent us from growing into the Men and Women of Christ God desires us to be. Like His Son who gave everything, we must be willing to give our all to grow to such noble character, but His Son's Atoning grace is the bridge that spans the chasm so that our "almost" is enough and sufficient to bring our imperfection into His perfection. Elder Hafen expressed it in these words:

> "So we must willingly give everything, because God Himself can't make us grow against our will and without our full participation. Yet even when we utterly spend ourselves, we lack the power to create the perfection only God can complete. Our *all* by itself is still only *almost* enough—until it is finished by the *all* of Him who is the 'finisher of our faith.'[23] At that point, our imperfect but consecrated *almost* is enough...
>
> "*Almost* is especially enough when our own sacrifices somehow echo the Savior's sacrifice, however imperfect we are."[48]

We must use such universalizing faith to "spend" ourselves in holiness, trying to become the embodiment of holiness, but not be discouraged when all we do just simply isn't enough, and won't ever be in this mortal life. Our perfection, our embodiment of holiness, and our absolute obedience will not be achieved in this life. Our perfection is pending.[49]

Summary

This chapter has focused on how early childhood experiences in one's family of origin shape how we perceive the characteristics and attributes of God, how attachment patterns in those families of origin influence attachment to God, and how developmental factors shape the type of faith one may develop.

The goal is not to lay the blame of scrupulosity on parents, nor to suggest that factors of development in faith and spirituality are the sole factors that contribute to the development of scrupulosity. Most people who develop scrupulosity would have developed some other form of OCD despite their experiences. But I have attempted to show how developmental factors in early life may have contributed to scrupulosity being the type of OCD one develops based on certain developmental characteristics (harsh, rigid parenting coupled with a similarly harsh, punitive religious training).

In my clinical work with those who struggle with scrupulosity, I have found it is usually very beneficial to address family of origin issues and to explore parent-child relationships, attachment styles, and trajectories of faith development that follow similar paths of human development (for example, Fowler's work relying on Piaget, Erickson, and Kohlberg). As they work through issues pertaining to their "God-attachment," stages of faith development, and other family of origin issues, they begin to see that scrupulous concerns may be rooted in factors other than purely spiritual matters. They can begin to see that something other than a battle between good and evil – the battle between God and the devil over their soul – may explain the obsessive thoughts and compulsive actions. They can begin to see that mental health concerns are at play and have reasonable explanations that point them toward healing human relationships within their family, reframing God in a more benevolent way, and finding compassion for themselves and others who struggle with scrupulosity. Most importantly, they begin to perceive that there is a way to embrace faith and overcome scrupulosity that will both bring them closer to God while healing from their mental illness – something most thought was impossible prior to treatment.

MINDFUL SELF-COMPASSION AND THE COMPASSION OF CHRIST

One of the most powerful emerging tools available in the field of therapy today is "mindful self-compassion." Drawing from Acceptance and Commitment Therapy (ACT – which we will discuss further in another chapter) and the work of scholars such as Kristen Neff, Kelly McGonigal, and others,[1] mindful self-compassion is a coping tool that can be easily taught and utilized. One typically uses mindful self-compassion when experiencing something emotionally difficult or troubling or after doing something that they regret (such as an addict who slips or relapses or a person trying to break the habit of procrastination but finds themselves falling back into the bad habit). The goal is to avoid toxically shaming one's self which often leads us back to faltering over and over cyclically.[2] It presupposes that guilt is behavior-focused while shame is focused on personhood or identity. Guilt may lead a person to think, "I made a mistake" whereas shame would lead one to conclude, "I am a mistake" (or "loser," "stupid," "worthless," etc.). Guilt can be a healthy way of responding to mistakes or sins because it focuses on changing behaviors. Shame, however, is unhealthy because it focuses on berating one's personhood or identity and does not lead to changes in behavior (and often perpetuates poor behavior). The goal of self-compassion is to eliminate shame, but it does not remove accountability for one's behaviors. It still allows for guilt, which includes an honest assessment of and accountability for one's mistakes, but does so in a way that puts the mistakes in a healthy perspective. Self-compassion has been found to be a healthy mediating variable to perfectionism.[3] Therefore, self-compassion can be applied to the scrupulous and address one of the key maladaptive beliefs that fuel OCD.

One study[4] found that those suffering with OCD may fear receiving compassion from others or from one's self, even though they are comfortable giving compassion to others. Recent research[5] has found there is a moderately strong negative or inverse correlation between self-compassion and OCD symptom severity, meaning that the more one uses self-compassion the symptoms of OCD begin to wane or abate. That same research, however, found that the effects of self-compassion on OCD symptom severity are mediated through emotional regulation difficulties. This means that self-compassion is most effective in influencing OCD symptoms if patients are also taught how to soothe or regulate their emotions and feelings. So, it is clear that for self-compassion to work as effectively as possible, patients also must be taught how to regulate their emotions, calm, themselves, and soothe their feelings of distress. The mindful self-compassion interventions suggested by Kristen Neff and others,[6] as well as the Mindful CBT and Mindfulness-Based Cognitive Therapy[7] that will be discussed in future chapters do just that – target emotional regulation as a means of enhancing the efficacy of self-compassion interventions.

Mindful self-compassion usually begins with taking a moment of internal thought or "self-dialogue" (thoughts that we think to ourselves, as if we are speaking to ourselves to calm ourselves down). Typically, one starts with taking a few deep breaths using the diaphragm and stomach muscles[8] and tries to focus only in the present moment rather than worrying about the past or the future. Then, once calm, the practitioner of mindful self-compassion focuses on three things:

1. Be mindful of the pain, emotion, or challenge you are experiencing in this moment. (Internal self-dialogue at this step often sounds like, "I'm really frustrated right now over what I just did or experienced" or "This is a moment of pain for me right now").
2. Remind yourself of the common humanity of the experience. (Internal self-dialogue at this step often sounds like, "I'm not the first person to struggle with this issue or pain. Others also suffer with this issue, and have overcome it, so maybe I can, too).
3. Give yourself an encouraging statement or expression that someone else who loves and cares about you would give if they were there to help you. (Internal self-dialogue at this step often sounds like, "My grandma would tell me not to give up hope, and I'll make it through this," "I should be as kind and gentle to myself as I would to a friend," or simply "I'm going to be okay – I can do this.")

Now it is important for the sufferer of scrupulosity to realize that mindful self-compassion isn't "rationalizing sin away" nor is it giving yourself a "pass" on things that need to be repented of (remember, scrupulosity is an anxiety-disorder, not a sin). Rather, it is a way to be a little more objective and less self-prosecutorial. The scrupulous are their own worst inner critics. Mindful self-compassion is simply a way to be fair with themselves rather than always erring on the side of being self-critical. Self-compassion can strengthen the scrupulous saint's positive self-view and self-worth, which is an important part of healing from OCD.[9]

Compassion for others and ourselves is rooted in Christ's nature and attributes. It is one of the defining characteristics of our Savior that most delineated Him from the rest of the world. Before Christ, most societies resembled Hobbes' famous description of the nature of life and humanity: "...continual fear and danger of a violent death, and the life of man, solitary, poor, nasty, brutish, and short."[10] Truly, most of world history shows the Adversary was successful in influencing people to make the mortal lives of their peers a miserable, merciless succession of selfishness and suffering – devoid of compassion and kindness on the whole. Cruelty, not compassion, is what people came to expect of the world. But when Christ came He showed compassion, love, healing, and hope.

It may be hard for modern people to understand the magnitude of difference Christ's teachings and example were in stark contrast to the norms of society in His day. Before the Savior's ministry (and even often afterward) most people eked out their existence where *maybe* they'd find some kindness in family and local friends, but it was not to be expected in general as a social norm. Sure, there were pockets of history where earlier prophets and others had been an exception or aberration from the norm of cruelty and carelessness – but they were truly rare and not widespread.

Christ's compassion was a defining characteristic that changed the world. His teachings systematized the practice of compassion and love, and His example of compassion and love is unparalleled. As Christians, we too, must strive to emulate Christ's charity, compassion, and kindness. Those virtues should be among the shining attributes of our being if we have inculcated His teachings within our hearts and lives. This is why this chapter on the subject of the compassion of Christ is so pertinent to the sufferer of scrupulosity. Whereas the Pharisees deserved every given rebuke for hypocrisy and self-promulgated, inflated haughtiness combined with arrogant self-righteousness (all the while failing to live the Gospel as the Great Lawgiver truly desired), the sufferers of scrupulosity deserve none of the same rebukes from the Master, nor would He be inclined to do so, in my opinion. Scrupulous members of the Church are more akin to the downtrodden, the mentally-assailed, and the outcasts that Christ freely healed and forgave with unbounding mercy and compassion. This chapter helps us explore this noble attribute of compassion of Christ to help the scrupulous to learn to be compassionate with others, but especially with themselves.

. . .

THE COMPASSION of Christ

Near the Easter celebration season, Latter-day Saints, like most Christians, reflect on the incidents that led to Christ's death and resurrection. The period from His triumphal entry into Jerusalem on a donkey as the Messiah and the events of the last week of His mortal life that ultimately lead up to His suffering in Gethsemane, His crucifixion on Golgotha, and His Resurrection on the third day from the Garden Tomb is often called in many Christian denominations – the "Passion of Christ." The Latin root of the word Passion is "pati-" – meaning to suffer or endure (as in the word "patience"), so it is appropriate to view the sufferings and death of Christ in that context as a Passion. The word Passion describes Christ's atoning suffering on our behalf.

We need to focus on the "*com*passion of Christ." Compassion adds to the root word of passion or suffering, the important prefix <u>*com*</u> meaning "<u>*with*</u>". Thus, compassion means to "**suffer <u>with</u>**" someone, and usually implies that such feelings of empathy for the suffering of others should move or motivate us to action. It is this definition of compassion I wish to use to better understand the "compassion" Christ has for each of us, and especially the sufferer of scrupulosity. By studying the "compassion of Christ" we can learn how Christ not only suffered *for* us but also suffers **with** us (and in many ways ***instead*** of us) as we strive to grow and progress in the Gospel. Such study may be helpful in ameliorating the suffering those struggling with scrupulosity often endure.

SCRIPTURAL ACCOUNTS of Christ's Compassion

Let's review a few scriptural accounts where the compassion of Christ is described. Many of these scriptures come from the New Testament but one important one also comes from Christ's visit to the Americas as recorded in the Book of Mormon. These examples illustrate the centrality of compassion as a key component of Christ's attributes and message.

. . .

Example #1

In Matthew chapter 14 we read about Christ teaching a multitude. They are out in the desert wilderness with no place to go eat. The hour grows late and Christ's apostles urge Him to send the crowd away to the nearby villages to obtain food. In the end, instead of sending them away, He feeds five thousand men as well as their women and children. But notice something else He does to manifest His compassion for them in addition to feeding them with five loaves and two fishes:

Matt. 14:14-21

> **14** And Jesus went forth, and saw a great multitude, and was moved with compassion toward them, and he healed their sick.
>
> **15** ¶ And when it was evening, his disciples came to him, saying, This is a desert place, and the time is now past; send the multitude away, that they may go into the villages, and buy themselves victuals.
>
> **16** But Jesus said unto them, They need not depart; give ye them to eat.
>
> **17** And they say unto him, We have here but five loaves, and two fishes.
>
> **18** He said, Bring them hither to me.
>
> **19** And he commanded the multitude to sit down on the grass, and took the five loaves, and the two fishes, and looking up to heaven, he blessed, and brake, and gave the loaves to his disciples, and the disciples to the multitude.
>
> **20** And they did all eat, and were filled: and they took up of the fragments that remained twelve baskets full.
>
> **21** And they that had eaten were about five thousand men, beside women and children.

Christ's compassion was not only for their temporary hunger needs, but He first healed many of them and then performed the miracle of the loaves and fishes. He cared about them in totality – their temporary hunger, but also their physical ailments and their spiritual souls, as well. He was not willing to send them away, but to show them that He would provide for them. Why? Because He was "moved with compassion towards them."

Example #2
Matt. 20:30-34

> 30 ¶ And, behold, two blind men sitting by the way side, when they heard that Jesus passed by, cried out, saying, Have mercy on us, O Lord, thou Son of David.
>
> 31 And the multitude rebuked them, because they should hold their peace: but they cried the more, saying, Have mercy on us, O Lord, thou Son of David.
>
> 32 And Jesus stood still, and called them, and said, What will ye that I shall do unto you?
>
> 33 They say unto him, Lord, that our eyes may be opened.
>
> 34 So Jesus had compassion on them, and touched their eyes: and immediately their eyes received sight, and they followed him.

Example #3
Mark 1:40-41

> 40 And there came a leper to him, beseeching him, and kneeling down to him, and saying unto him, If thou wilt, thou canst make me clean.

41 And Jesus, moved with compassion, put forth his hand, and touched him, and saith unto him, I will; be thou clean.

In both examples two and three described above, Christ was "moved with compassion" to heal, but notice how Christ only did so after they cried out to Him and beseeched Him. The Savior is a responsive Messiah. While others in the multitude told the two blind men to essentially shut their mouths and quit calling out to the Master, Christ responded to their pleas, asked what it was that *they* desired of Him and had compassion on them because of their suffering. Christ had tremendous empathy for their suffering and responded with great kindness, compassion, and mercy. By this we may know that He will hear and respond to our cries, pleas, and prayers as we petition Him in faith.

Example # 4
Luke 7:11-15

11 ¶ And it came to pass the day after, that he went into a city called Nain; and many of his disciples went with him, and much people.

12 Now when he came nigh to the gate of the city, behold, there was a dead man carried out, the only son of his mother, and she was a widow: and much people of the city was with her.

13 And when the Lord saw her, he had compassion on her, and said unto her, Weep not.

14 And he came and touched the bier: and they that bare him stood still. And he said, Young man, I say unto thee, Arise.

15 And he that was dead sat up, and began to speak. And he delivered him to his mother.

In this example we see how Christ noticed the needs of a suffering woman and was obedient to the baptismal covenant we all make to "mourn with those that mourn." But Jesus did more than just mourn with her, He took action – action that was within His power – to meet the widow's need. As a widow with no husband, she would have had no support except whatever support her children would give to her. With the death of her son – her *only* son – she would likely be bereft of all her support financially and emotionally. The Lord, in His wisdom, deemed that the son was needed more in Nain than in the spirit world and brought him back to the widow of Nain to support his mother. It also seemed to portend or foretell the coming event when *God's Only Begotten Son* would use this same power over life and death to rise from the dead to bring about the resurrection of us all, but not merely to bring the dead back to a mortal life (as was the case of the widow of Nain's son) but to immortality and eternal life.

Example #5

3 Nephi 17:5-10

5 And it came to pass that when Jesus had thus spoken, he cast his eyes round about again on the multitude, and beheld they were in tears, and did look steadfastly upon him as if they would ask him to tarry a little longer with them.

6 And he said unto them: Behold, my bowels are filled with compassion towards you.

7 Have ye any that are sick among you? Bring them hither. Have ye any that are lame, or blind, or halt, or maimed, or leprous, or that are withered, or that are deaf, or that are afflicted in any manner? Bring them hither and I will heal them, for I have compassion upon you; my bowels are filled with mercy.

8 For I perceive that ye desire that I should show unto you what I have done unto your brethren at Jerusalem, for I see that your faith is sufficient that I should heal you.

9 And it came to pass that when he had thus spoken, all the multitude, with one accord, did go forth with their sick and their afflicted, and their lame, and with their blind, and with their dumb, and with all them that were afflicted in any manner; and he did heal them every one as they were brought forth unto him.

10 And they did all, both they who had been healed and they who were whole, bow down at his feet, and did worship him; and as many as could come for the multitude did kiss his feet, insomuch that they did bathe his feet with their tears.

NOTICE HOW CHRIST knew they needed more time to process the things He had taught them earlier that day and so He prepared to go and fulfill other assignments from the Father. But He was attuned to the "God-attachment" needs of the people. They wanted Him to tarry a little longer and not feel abandoned. Sensing their need, He provided a way to linger with them, bless them, and have mercy on them. He was once again motivated by His compassion for them. In fact, He described this inner yearning of empathic love and understanding of their situation as having His "bowels filled with compassion." His compassion was felt at the deepest level within His soul. These examples (and many, many more) show that Christ's most consistent attribute was deep levels of compassion for those around Him that suffered.

Moved to Compassion Motivated to Act

Notice a pattern in all five of these passages recounted above. In each account, we see the Savior having empathy, mercy, and compassion for the suffering of others. He is "moved with compassion." This compassion "moves" Him to act to relieve the suffering of others. Notice how this compassion is described as filling His bowels. It is a feeling so deep and so inherent within the soul that it is best described as a yearning to help others at the core inside of us.

It is an inherent trait of compassion that it "moves" or motivates us to act. When we see the suffering of others and are full of compassion, we can't keep from helping the sufferer. So it is with Heavenly Father and Jesus Christ. Recall what Elder Jeffrey R. Holland taught regarding their compassionate nature:

> "Just because God is God, just because Christ is Christ, they cannot do other than care for us and bless us and help us if we will but come unto them, approaching their throne of grace in meekness and lowliness of heart. They can't help but bless us. They have to. It is their nature."[11]

Compassion is a motivating force to do good. God and His Son are the full embodiment of the virtue of compassion. If we are to become like God, we must embrace compassion – compassion for others and for ourselves. This compassion must motivate us to act. This is important to understand compassion's motivating force to do good because it is necessary to see self-compassion in the same light for the sufferer of scrupulosity. They must learn to *act* in ways that will alleviate their suffering. We shall discuss this further in a future chapter when we discuss Acceptance and Commitment Therapy (ACT).

Christ's Atonement Allows Him to Suffer For Us, Suffer With Us, and Suffer Instead of Us – Why? Because He Loves Us and Has Compassion on Us

When we consider the "compassion of Christ" we might be interested in exploring how Christ's Atonement allows Him to suffer *for* us, suffer *with* us, and (in some instances) suffer *instead* of us. How does His compassion, as an inherent Godly attribute, help us understand our relationship to our Heavenly Father as a loving, compassionate Being?

For example, how comprehensive is the Savior's Atonement? In all honesty whole volumes of books have been written on the subject and every time, the writer feels they come up short of describing the Atonement of Christ. Why? Because His atoning sacrifice is *infinite*.[12] One cannot ever come close to describing all of the aspects of this infinite Atonement wrought by the Master. But the prophet Alma the Younger points us in the direction of comprehending that the Savior's atoning sacrifice was not only for sin, but for illnesses, pains, afflictions, and suffering of every kind in Alma 7:11-12.

> 11 And he shall go forth, suffering pains and afflictions and temptations of every kind; and this that the word might be fulfilled which saith he will take upon him the pains and the sicknesses of his people.
>
> 12 And he will take upon him death, that he may loose the bands of death which bind his people; and he will take upon him their infirmities, that his bowels may be filled with mercy, according to the flesh, that he may know according to the flesh how to succor his people according to their infirmities.

THE SUFFERING of every sin and the suffering of every victim of sin; the suffering of every illness (including mental illnesses like scrupulosity); the suffering anguish of every pain, broken bone, sunburn, cancer, and disease; the emotional suffering of every heartbreak, disappointment, death, loss, and abandonment; the suffering caused by weaknesses and imperfections that do not rise to the level of sin, but are still architects of sorrow and regret; in fine, the suffering from every negative and miserable human experience that ever has occurred or every will occur was part of the "awful arithmetic of the Atonement" of Jesus Christ which He suffered for us in Gethsemane and again on Calvary or Golgotha. There is no miserable human experience in all the history of the world that Christ did not experience to the fullest degree and completely and abundantly pay the price for. The scriptures testify that this is true, and all I can do is add my witness that this is true, though it is a staggering concept to comprehend. *Christ suffered for all of us!* I am humbled and deeply grateful that He did.

But here is the miracle of it all for me. Does He now stand back and say, "Okay, I suffered for it, so now you are on your own as you experience some of those miserable experiences, illnesses, and sins of mortality"? Absolutely not! Christ stands with open arms as we suffer and will suffer **with** us here and now as we sojourn on our mortal journey back to Heavenly Father. He suffers **with** us every step of the way and eases our yokes and burdens. In Matthew 11: 28-30 we read:

> 28 ¶ Come unto me, all ye that labour and are heavy laden, and I will give you rest.
>
> 29 Take my yoke upon you, and learn of me; for I am meek and lowly in heart: and ye shall find rest unto your souls.
>
> 30 For my yoke is easy, and my burden is light.

WE ARE NOT LEFT ALONE to suffer through mortality unaided. The Savior not only suffered for us in the past, He suffers now *with* us every step of the way. He is acquainted with our situations, scrupulosity, sufferings, sins, and sorrows, because He has borne them and now uses that familiarity with our afflictions as a resource to succor us in our present hour of need. The prophet Isaiah taught:

> 4 ¶ Surely he hath borne our griefs, and carried our sorrows: yet we did esteem him stricken, smitten of God, and afflicted.

5 But he was wounded for our transgressions, he was bruised for our iniquities: the chastisement of our peace was upon him; and with his stripes we are healed. (Isaiah 53:4-5)

In some cases, Christ suffers *with* us and in other special cases He suffers *instead* of us. As a Melchizedek priesthood holder, I have been privileged to lay hands on the sick (either physically or mentally ill) and pronounce the Lord's blessing upon them. In some cases, the illness remains and the Savior suffers *with* or alongside the afflicted person – not taking the sickness away – but allowing the suffering through sickness to be instructive and formative in some ways known only to God and the sufferer in the spiritual journey of the individual. I know that in those instances where the illness has not been removed, the Savior still provided "tender mercies" which aided or comforted the afflicted person.

In other instances, the Lord chooses to suffer the sickness or illness *instead* of the afflicted individual. Because He already suffered the sickness or affliction in Gethsemane and Golgotha, He deems that the suffering soul need not endure the sorrowful suffering. I don't know why in some instances He suffers with us and in other ones He suffers instead of us. Maybe, the suffering would not lead to the tailor-made spiritual development of the person, or maybe simply because He desires to alleviate as much pain as He can without depriving the individual of some necessary learning. Possibly there could be many more reasons in His reckoning. Usually such intimate knowledge is between God and the sufferer. But I have seen people immediately healed as a result of a priesthood blessing and know that because the Savior experienced that affliction as part of His Atonement, He had power to take that illness away through the power of the priesthood. In some instances, He suffers *instead* of us.

There is one sacred area of mortality where Christ freely offers to suffer in our stead. That is the area of sin and repentance. Now don't get me wrong: It doesn't mean that consequences of sinful choices don't sometimes remain for instructive redemptive purposes. But

Christ does offer that through repentance He will suffer the price of sin instead of us:

> **15** Therefore I command you to repent—repent, lest I smite you by the rod of my mouth, and by my wrath, and by my anger, and your sufferings be sore—how sore you know not, how exquisite you know not, yea, how hard to bear you know not.
>
> **16** For behold, I, God, have suffered these things for all, that they might not suffer if they would repent;
>
> **17** But if they would not repent they must suffer even as I;
>
> **18** Which suffering caused myself, even God, the greatest of all, to tremble because of pain, and to bleed at every pore, and to suffer both body and spirit—and would that I might not drink the bitter cup, and shrink—
>
> **19** Nevertheless, glory be to the Father, and I partook and finished my preparations unto the children of men.
>
> **20** Wherefore, I command you again to repent, lest I humble you with my almighty power; and that you confess your sins, lest you suffer these punishments of which I have spoken, of which in the smallest, yea, even in the least degree you have tasted at the time I withdrew my Spirit. (Doctrine and Covenants 19:15-20)

WE MUST LEARN TO "SUFFER WITH" Others and Ourselves Compassionately

I've come to learn through life experiences, through my work as a therapist, and through my service as a bishop that *everyone* suffers. We need to be compassionate and suffer with others utilizing Christ-like charity, compassion, and love. Whether we mourn the death of a loved one, suffer with a health condition (including scrupulosity), worry about wayward children, or simply struggle with a sense of despair or inadequacy due to failings, sins, and weaknesses, we can all follow the Savior's example to "succor the weak, lift up the hands which hang down, and strengthen the feeble knees." In Doctrine and Covenants 81:4-5 we read:

> **4** And in doing these things thou wilt do the greatest good unto thy fellow beings, and wilt promote the glory of him who is your Lord.
>
> **5** Wherefore, be faithful; stand in the office which I have appointed unto you; succor the weak, lift up the hands which hang down, and strengthen the feeble knees.

It is helpful for the scrupulous to learn that the "greatest good" is to be compassionate to others and to themselves. Compassion to others and to one's self is a much greater good than condemning others or being self-condemning. More good will come to the scrupulous as they are self-compassionate rather than self-prosecutorial.

Often, we see young adult men and women either come home early from a mission or not able to serve a mission at all due to their mental health. As a young missionary I knew of several elders who I now recognize must have been suffering with scrupulosity, though I did not know about the mental illness at the time. Life on a mission was very painful for them. We must learn that those who return home early from a mission (whether it be for honorable reasons such as medical and mental health concerns or for less than honorable reasons) are suffering and need our support and compassion, rather than judgment. They must learn to be self-compassionate to themselves, as well. Even for those who never serve a mission, there is a place for them in the Church and kingdom of God. I've known young adult men who have felt "less than" (discrepancy) because they didn't serve a mission for whatever reason. We need to do a better job of helping all to feel welcome regardless of their history. The Gospel is a "wide net" with "many kinds of fish," so to speak. There is room for all who love the Lord and want the Atonement of Christ to be effective in their lives. For those who are less active, have become disaffected, or who otherwise feel marginalized, we must reach out through compassionate, personal ministries of those of us who are currently blessed to feel we belong here.

As we develop charity, love, and compassion for others, we will better emulate the Savior and be moved to action to care for the struggling, suffering, poor, and otherwise needy. This is also true for the scrupulous who engage in self-compassion – they will develop strength through their struggles and faith that is not fraught with fear.

How can we better follow Christ's example and be more compassionate with others around us who suffer? May I suggest three things.

1. Covenants Helps us to Have Compassion

First of all, covenants and covenant keeping is one vital way to develop greater compassion.

In the baptismal covenants we made we promised the following:

8 And it came to pass that he said unto them: Behold, here are the waters of Mormon (for thus were they called) and now, as ye are desirous to come into the fold of God, and to be called his people, and are willing to bear one another's burdens, that they may be light;

9 Yea, and are willing to mourn with those that mourn; yea, and comfort those that stand in need of comfort, and to stand as witnesses of God at all times and in all things, and in all places that ye may be in, even until death, that ye may be redeemed of God, and be numbered with those of the first resurrection, that ye may have eternal life—

10 Now I say unto you, if this be the desire of your hearts, what have you against being baptized in the name of the Lord, as a witness before him that ye have entered into a covenant with him, that ye will serve him and keep his commandments, that he may pour out his Spirit more abundantly upon you? (Mosiah 18:8-10)

The capstone covenants in the temple include what is called the Abrahamic covenant. Notice what the Old Testament says about God's compassion towards those who fall under the Abrahamic covenant:

> 23 And the Lord was gracious unto them, and had compassion on them, and had respect unto them, because of his covenant with Abraham, Isaac, and Jacob, and would not destroy them, neither cast he them from his presence as yet. (2 Kings 13:23)

In the temple we are invited into the presence of the Lord. Through making and keeping sacred temple covenants we will develop a ministerial attitude of compassion toward our fellow men and women. The blessings of the Gospel flow into the lives of his descendants (all of us) so that we can work towards the "perfecting of saints." Then the promise of the Abrahamic covenant continues so that through Abraham's seed the remaining families of the earth would be blessed with the Gospel blessings (see Abr. 2:8-11). As we understand the blessings of the Abrahamic covenant, we are first blessed to have the Gospel in our own lives and then we are "moved with compassion" to assist the remaining families of the earth to enjoy the blessings of the Gospel through missionary and temple work. For the Latter-day Saint who suffers with scrupulosity, they must begin to realize that God's covenants with them through our father Abraham are meant to pour down grace, compassion, and respect on them such that they can trust they will not be destroyed or cast out from His presence (see 2 Kings 13:23). He will be extremely merciful to them because of the Abrahamic covenant, of which they are recipients.

2. Pray for the Pure Love of Christ – His Charity and Compassion
In addition to covenants, praying for spiritual gifts is another

powerful tool to receive the grace and gifts of God. Praying for the compassion for self and others is a good thing for the scrupulous. In Moroni 7:47-48 we read:

> 47 But charity is the pure love of Christ, and it endureth forever; and whoso is found possessed of it at the last day, it shall be well with him.
>
> 48 Wherefore, my beloved brethren, pray unto the Father with all the energy of heart, that ye may be filled with this love, which he hath bestowed upon all who are true followers of his Son, Jesus Christ; that ye may become the sons of God; that when he shall appear we shall be like him, for we shall see him as he is; that we may have this hope; that we may be purified even as he is pure. Amen.

3. We Must Be Moved with Compassion to Serve Others

Finally, taking action is imperative to truly be compassionate. Compassion is not just a feeling – it is an action. Compassion motivates us to care for the poor, needy, sick, afflicted and anyone else who is suffering. The Lord desires that the sufferer of scrupulosity learn to apply that same motivated, compassionate actions towards themselves. In Doctrine and Covenants 52:40 we read:

> 40 And remember in all things the poor and the needy, the sick and the afflicted, for he that doeth not these things, the same is not my disciple.

To truly be a disciple of Christ, the Latter-day Saint must have compassion for others and for themselves. Scrupulosity and OCD are a mental illness and so they must begin to see themselves as among the "sick and afflicted" group of people that the Lord commands all of His disciples to be compassionate towards. That is why self-compassion for the scrupulous is mandatory if they truly wish to follow God's laws and be His disciple.

How the Scrupulous Can Practice Mindful Self-Compassion

Hopefully, this chapter has convinced the reader of the necessity of compassion, including self-compassion, as an essential attribute to be a disciple of Jesus Christ. For the scrupulous who may be reading this and want to know more about how to practice mindful self-compassion may I remind you of a few basic steps and then point you to some resources to further assist you. Remember to engage in a few minutes of mindful self-compassion at least once or twice a day (more often may be needed, so long as it doesn't become a new compulsion to replace other ones like prayer or other rituals may have become in your life). Start by engaging in diaphragmatic breathing to calm yourself and regulate your emotions. Then remember the three key elements of self-compassion: being mindful of the pain or emotion in the moment, recognizing our common humanity, and giving yourself positive encouragement. Some even choose to use a physical, soothing gesture during a self-compassion break. Physical touch releases oxytocin – a natural biochemical – into our system. So discretely rubbing or caressing your arm, placing your hand over your heart in a loving way, or any other appropriate form of physical self-touch that is caring and soothing can be added to the self-compassion break. Remember the goal here is to be as gentle and compassionate to one's self as we would be to a friend. Using a tone of voice (yes, even silent mental thoughts to one's self can have different tones from kind to accusatory), giving a hug, holding a hand, or simply listening with love the way you would normally do to others is how you need to learn to engage with yourself through mindful self-compassion.

There are many resources to assist you with mindful self-compassion, including apps that you can download onto your phone to guide your through meditations or self-compassion breaks (See the Appendix for a list of resources regarding mindful self-compassion).

PHASE II: COGNITIVE BEHAVIORAL THERAPY TREATMENTS FOR OCD AND SCRUPULOSITY

Preliminaries of Phase II: Medication Consideration and Strategic Paradoxes

Medication Consideration

One of the most important things to ensure in therapy is that anyone suffering from any mental illness (depression, anxiety, OCD, or others) receive a physical exam from a competent medical doctor. There are some medical conditions that may appear with symptoms similar to a mental illness (for example, hypothyroidism and depression have similar features). It is necessary to have a medical professional rule out any medical causes for the symptoms.

It is also useful to have a competent medical doctor (usually a psychiatrist) evaluate the patient to determine if, and what kind of, medications may help with scrupulosity/OCD. The International Obsessive-Compulsive Disorder Foundation (IOCDF) estimates that "about 7 out of 10 people with OCD will benefit from medication or Exposure and Response Prevention (ERP). For the people who benefit from medication, they usually see their OCD symptoms reduced by 40-60%."[1]

. . .

Strategic Paradoxes

Do you remember Aaron[2*] from the Introduction of this book – the young man who wanted to serve a mission but his scrupulosity compulsion was to pray repetitively and excessively? He was pretty resistant to most therapy interventions I used with him at first. But one day, he came into our session – late as usual – because he was trying to pray "just right." I was inspired to explore a rather strategic, paradoxical intervention with him (this was in the middle of the treatment plan long after we had joined and established a therapeutic alliance or relationship of trust). I asked him about Alma's prayer in Alma chapter 31 when he saw the Zoramites praying on the Rameumtom. The Zoramites used a set prayer with just the right words (according to their beliefs) but Alma's prayer (in contrast to the Zoramites) was very heartfelt and informal. I asked him to contrast Alma's prayer with a typical Latter-day Saint prayer. I pointed out several ways Alma's prayer isn't the typical "Mormon prayer" we are used to in our culture. Alma doesn't directly address Heavenly Father in prayer (Alma just starts talking like he is talking to a Friend – "O, how long, O Lord,…); he doesn't follow the standard "give thanks first and then ask for your needs second" admonition we gave as missionaries to investigators first learning to pray; and Alma doesn't close in the name of Jesus Christ as we typically do in our faith. Alma's prayer doesn't follow *any* conventional formula at all – but it is heartfelt and beautiful nonetheless. After reviewing all of the ways Alma's prayer doesn't follow the conventional norm, I then asked Aaron the strategic question, "Do you think God heard Alma's prayer?" This strategic question was a paradoxical bind for Aaron. There was no way to dispute that God heard Alma's prayer. After all, Alma was a prophet. The scriptural account goes on to indicate that Alma did another unconventional thing (clapping his hands upon his fellow missionaries), and they were filled with the Holy Ghost. So obviously God heard this prophet's very informal, unconventional prayer and blessed Alma and his companions in spite of Alma not praying "just right" according to our standards of prayer. But from Aaron's perspective, how could that be? How could God answer such an unconventional prayer? What does that mean for praying "just right" as a way of perfecting prayer?

I wanted Aaron to be caught in this strategic paradox for that very reason. He needed to come face to face with the absurdity and illogical nature of his perfectionistic compulsion. He needed to be put in a bind, so to speak, so he'd have to cognitively re-examine his previously unexamined assumption that following prayer conventions "just right" would lead to greater spiritual power in his life. And, if he didn't "feel"[3*] powerful spiritual and emotional relief following his prayer, he assumed he must be doing his compulsion (praying) wrong somehow, so he would need to repeat it over and over until he felt some kind of relief that he interpreted as the Spirit or spiritual power in his life. These assumptions and compulsions systemically and recursively contributed to his OCD and needed to be challenged and re-examined. The strategic use of paradox forced Aaron to begin this much needed re-examination so that he could take a different approach in treatment.

This moment in therapy really "broke the case wide open" for Aaron and was a significant first step towards his eventual growth and healing from scrupulosity to the degree he was able to serve and complete a faithful mission. It forced him to question his obsessive-compulsive assumptions and really dig deeper into his mental health and reasoning. It was also a huge learning experience for me as a therapist beginning to clinically work with scrupulosity.

It seems that the nature of OCD is inherently paradoxical. As we will learn in subsequent chapters, the more the person with OCD tries to fight their obsessions with avoidance patterns or compulsive rituals, the worse their condition gets. Thus, paradoxical interventions are often needed. While many treatment techniques that we will be exploring in subsequent chapters – such as ERP and ACT – have commonly used paradoxes, I have come to believe that I need to discover and develop tailor-made "strategic paradoxes" in treating scrupulosity. This is one of the reasons why an LDS client or patient with scrupulosity needs to work with a Latter-day Saint clinician or at least someone who is intimately familiar with our religion and culture. I have come to believe that the clinician needs to establish their "religious authority" as someone who is orthodox and will not lead the scrupulous astray. They need someone they trust who is faithful in the Gospel when the clinician intervenes using strategic paradoxes that cause them to question their fundamental assumptions that are rooted in OCD (but the scrupulous see them as rooted in their faith). This cognitive reframing must be done in a relational context where the client will not perceive such questioning as questioning the tenets of the faith, but rather exploring newer and more insightful ways to embrace the faith that are also healthier for them mentally. In working with each client, I strive to look for tailor-made ways that address their central obsessive-compulsive issue and devise a unique strategic paradox that will cause them to have to come face to face with the bind forcing them to rethink and revalue their old ways of thinking in obsessive-compulsive ways. I seek to help them embrace new elements of their faith that will lead to better mental health while questioning erroneous assumption they have about their faith all the while helping them feel secure that letting go of the parts that are hurting them won't jeopardize their soul. By embracing Gospel truths, they can let go and overcome the scrupulosity as they come to healthier understandings of the Gospel and of how mental illness works.

Sometimes, the scrupulous are so rigid in their thinking that it takes powerful interventions to loosen their rigid adherence to their interpretations of Gospel living practices that aren't necessarily rooted in doctrine but in tradition and misunderstanding. For example, with Lisa,[4*] the woman who would pray incessantly including praying for long periods of time in public bathrooms, she felt compelled to "pray always" to avoid the temptations of the devil as instructed by the Savior in 3 Nephi 18:15. So when she saw people (including cartoon characters) kiss she would pray to resist the temptation of lust. Inevitably, she was praying for hours and hours on end. I devised a praying schedule with her (because not praying at all would not be an option nor desirable). Using Amulek's counsel in Alma 34: 21, we set up a time that she would formally engage in kneeling, verbal prayer in the "morning, mid-day, and evening." This would limit her prayer time to only three times a day for no more than an hour or less each. At the other times, she would have to face her fears and anxieties without resorting to her compulsion. It is true that she could still engage informal mental prayers where her heart was "full, drawn out in prayer" (see Alma 34:27) when she was not formally crying out to God in prayer, but the scripture implies that the person is actively doing something other than prayer all the while (Alma 34:17-27 speaks of praying for others in their household, flocks, fields, crops, etc. and implies that the person doing the praying is working in these endeavors all day long). So, I gave her a directive whereby she could only engage in any informal, silent prayers while she was actively doing something. I then talked to her about how she should limit the praying to specific, active purposes rather than simply praying compulsively for relief or deliverance from temptation. She had to institute active behaviors in the place of paralyzing prayer. It wasn't the full step toward response prevention used in ERP (which we will discuss later in the next chapter), but it was a starting point for where she was at and a baby step towards change. By strategically linking mental prayer with action, I was striving to get her to be prepared for the four step regimen that Jeffrey Schwartz, M.D. uses in his books *Brain Lock* and *You are Not Your Brain*.[5]

Dr. Jeffrey Schwartz *and the Four Step Regimen*

Dr. Jeffrey Schwartz is a neuroscientist and Research Psychiatrist at the UCLA School of Medicine. His book *Brain Lock*[6] is one of the first readings I suggest to patients suffering from OCD. In a concise and readily understandable way, Dr. Schwartz explains how OCD works in the brain and what steps a patient can take to change the patterns of obsessions and compulsions. Dr. Schwartz defines obsessions as "intrusive, unwelcome, distressing thoughts and mental images" and teaches patients to label them as "deceptive brain messages."[7] He defines compulsions as "...the behaviors that people with OCD perform in a vain attempt to exorcise the fears and anxieties caused by their obsessions," and he goes on to explain that the person with OCD most often logically "... recognizes that the urge to wash, check, or touch things or to repeat numbers is ridiculous and senseless" but becomes overwhelmed by the obsession that they eventually give in and engage in the compulsive behavior.[8] Dr. Schwartz's research suggests:

> "We now know that OCD is related to a biochemical problem in the brain. We call this problem 'Brain Lock' because four key structures of the brain become locked together, and the brain starts sending false messages that the person cannot readily recognize as false. One of the main signal-processing centers of the brain, made up of two structures called the *caudate nucleus* and the *putamen,* can be thought of as similar to a gearshift in a car. The caudate nucleus works like an automatic transmission for the front, or thinking part, of the brain. Working with the putamen, which is the automatic transmission for the part of the brain that controls body movements, the caudate nucleus allows for the extremely efficient coordination of thought and movement during everyday activities. In a person with OCD, however, the caudate nucleus is not shifting the gears properly, and messages from the front part of the brain get stuck there. In other words, the brain's automatic transmission has a glitch. The brain gets 'stuck in gear' and can't shift to the next thought."[9]

The good news is that mindfulness-based Cognitive-Behavioral Therapy (CBT) can help a person with OCD (including scrupulosity) to gradually, but literally, change their brain and get the brain's "transmission" to heal, repair, and begin to function smoother. Dr. Schwartz's approach begins by utilizing four steps involving four "R's" which help guide a person with OCD through the cognitive and behavioral changes they need to overcome OCD. By consistently applying the four steps, the person with OCD/scrupulosity can change how they respond to the obsessions and eventually progress to healing and changing how their brain works. The four steps are:

1. Relabel
2. Reattribute/Reframe[10*]
3. Refocus
4. Revalue

Relabeling deceptive brain messages can be difficult at first. But recognizing that some thoughts are just annoying noise and others are useful information is an important distinction for someone with OCD to make. That thoughts can be deceptive and not of value is often a new concept for the sufferer of scrupulosity. Labeling the intrusive thoughts as false, deceptive brain messages is the first step to recovery. Patients should not do this in a casual way. Using what is often called the "Impartial Spectator" (the objective perspective one can take to observe their thoughts and actions), a person with OCD can assertively and firmly relabel the thought or urge for what they really are: an obsession or compulsion. Taking a firm stance that what one is experiencing (without trying to make it go away) is indeed an obsession or compulsive urge helps the patient squarely address the issue. By calling it what it really is, they can recognize that the thoughts and feelings are really a false alarm.

Secondly, in therapy I teach the patient to reattribute or reframe the thought as coming from a different source than they have previously thought. Most scrupulous saints assume that the intrusive thoughts and feelings of guilt come from the Holy Ghost, and that God is telling them that they are not worthy or have not fully repented "just right." The reattribution/reframe step helps the person to consider a new source of those thoughts and feelings – their OCD/scrupulosity – not a spiritual message from God. As they begin to reframe the question of the source of their unpleasant, obsessive thoughts and feelings and attribute the feelings to their mental illness, they begin to find a powerful tool to refute the obsessions. I teach them to mentally state to themselves, "It's not me; it's my OCD" or "It's not me; it's my scrupulosity" or even "It's not me; it's my brain" based on the example given in Dr. Schwartz's *Brain Lock* from one of his patients (Dottie) who first coined the phrase, "It's not me – it's my OCD."[11]

The third step – refocusing – can often be one of the most challenging steps in this process because it requires the sufferer of OCD to purposely shift their focus and actions to something other than their obsessions and compulsions *even while continuing to feel the anxiety and pressure created by those obsessions and the need to engage in the compulsive behavior.* The patient has to force themselves to think and do something else even though the obsessive thoughts are still bothering them and the urge to act out a compulsion is still strong. Engaging in some wholesome task or activity that redirects the thoughts and actions of the sufferer away from the obsessions and compulsions creates a buffer of space and time so that they can eventually engage in the fourth step.

After the obsessive feelings, thoughts, and urges have subsided (which takes longer and is extremely hard at first, but gets quicker and easier over many, many times), the scrupulous sufferer can begin to revalue those earlier scrupulous thoughts and feelings from a clearer perspective. They can see the obsessions and compulsive urges for what they are – aspects of their OCD that they need not place any credence or value in.

Using the Four Step regimen – Relabel, Reattribute/Reframe, Refocus, and Revalue can be a very effective initial intervention for the scrupulous. In fact, Dr. Schwartz's research suggests that the effectiveness of this form of treatment is so powerful that the brain is literally changed and healed through this process.[12] In fact, Dr. Schwartz's research found through PET scans of the brains of OCD patients that the energy or activity levels of the caudate nucleus was reduced through a ten-week program using his four-step regimen. Reduced energy or activity in the caudate nucleus would indicate less obsessions – less thoughts getting stuck or "locked" in that part of the brain. In as short as ten weeks, we can see tremendous improvement simply by utilizing the Four Step regimen developed by Dr. Schwartz.

. . .

MINDFULNESS-BASED COGNITIVE THERAPY (MBCT) and other Cognitive Therapy Approaches

Similarly, other mindfulness-based interventions (MBIs) have shown promising results with mental health issues in general,[13] and with OCD in particular.[14] Mindfulness-based Cognitive Therapy (MBCT) is based off the concept that there are multiple psychological modes of receiving and processing information emotionally and cognitively. These modes or "Interacting Cognitive Subsystems"[15] have several different foci, and among those modes one is focused on "doing/acting" and another on "being." The theory is that the doing/acting mode is very task-driven and that the patient sees the discrepancy between "what is" and what they want things to be like. This discrepancy is part of the negative cognitive process that leads to mental health issues. By teaching the patient to switch to the "being" mode, they can come to accept "what is" and not feel the negative emotions from discrepancy. And, as noted earlier, "discrepancy" is a major contributor to the mental and affective processes of scrupulosity.[16] Mindfulness is also a major component of Acceptance and Commitment Therapy (ACT) which will be addressed further in a subsequent chapter.

MBCT is an 8-week group training program that involves meditation, cognitive reappraisal ability,[17] and exercises that enhance mindfulness. Some of those exercises include asking the patient to mindfully use their five senses while eating a raisin, engaging in a body scan, walking in the outdoors while meditating, practicing yoga, engaging in breathing exercises (including diaphragmatic breathing that is excellent for calming a patient's nervous systems), and progressive muscle relaxation. While it may not always be possible in a private practice setting to have group therapy (or the patient may not be amenable to a group setting for their treatment), the exercises and lessons from MBCT may still be utilized individually to significant benefit.

Other cognitive therapy (CT) approaches that do not utilize MBCT or ERP have attempted to directly address the cognitive schemas and maladaptive beliefs that fuel OCD. One fascinating study[18] of a 24-week CT treatment found that alleviation of OCD symptom severity was improved in correspondence with a decrease in perfectionism and increase in tolerance for uncertainty. Such promising results for directly focusing treatment on maladaptive beliefs and schemas strengthens the main thesis of this SOS model that adding an element of addressing belief systems in addition to ERP and ACT is an important step for increasing the efficacy of treatment of people with scrupulosity.

Though some proponents of other models of treatment may express concern about the use of mindfulness in treatment approaches,[19] others, including the leading scholar in the field of Exposure and Response Prevention (ERP) for scrupulosity – Dr. Jonathan S. Abramowitz, have appeared to have embraced it within their recommended treatment modalities and publications.[20] It would seem that integrating other models and elements with ERP is a growing recent trend in the field of treating OCD. But let's more closely examine the "gold standard" of OCD treatment – Exposure and Response Prevention (ERP) – and explore this important step in the SOS model.

EXPOSURE AND RESPONSE PREVENTION AND SCRUPULOSITY

*E*xposure and Response Prevention or ERP is the most widely used intervention for OCD. ERP has been shown to be effective in overcoming OCD from about 50-60%[1] of the time in one study by a leading expert of that approach to as high as 60-85%[2] of the time by another scholar. That is why any treatment model of scrupulosity should include ERP. Yet, other studies show that 25% of people suffering with OCD refuse to engage in ERP treatment, another 20% do not respond when receiving ERP, and yet again another 20% who do respond well during treatment relapse after treatment.[3] [4] Furthermore, some scholars argue that treatment of religious obsessions is even more difficult to treat with ERP and medication than other subtypes,[5] and scrupulosity patients show poorer treatment responses.[6] Yet, despite these difficulties, ERP remains an essential component of treatment for Latter-day Saints with scrupulosity, provided it is done by a competent therapist with a clear understanding of LDS beliefs, customs, and practices.

In the earlier portion of the 20th century, most psychologists used Freudian approaches to treatment. As Freudian approaches seemed to have little effect on treating OCD, most clinicians felt OCD was untreatable. Historically, one of the first behavioral-oriented psychologists to apply ERP techniques to OCD patients was Dr. Victor Meyer who worked at a psychiatric hospital in England in the 1960s.[7] Using "flooding interventions," Dr. Meyer exposed his patients with obsessions about contamination to the very things they feared without allowing them to wash or perform any cleaning rituals. Mentally, the patients felt they were staying "contaminated" for a long period of time and would experience high anxiety, but over time they began to feel the anxiety subside and realized the things they feared (illness or death through contamination) did not occur. This process was repeated daily for a few months so that they could eventually feel safe even though they may still experience the intrusive thought or urge. Word of Dr. Meyer's successes spread worldwide, and clinics began utilizing ERP to treat OCD. Thus was born the first-line of treatment options for OCD. Even today, ERP remains the leading form of treatment for OCD with the most demonstrable outcome effects.

Today, Cognitive Behavioral Therapy in general, and ERP in particular, is very detailed in its approach to OCD treatment. This approach outlines three components of an obsession – triggers, obsessional intrusions, and feared consequences.[8] Triggers could come in the form of any situation, person, object, or experience that "prompts unwanted obsessional thoughts, anxiety, or distress."[9] An obsessional intrusion is the thought, urge, image, or impulse itself. Feared consequences are the unwanted outcomes that the patient fears will happen if they don't avoid the trigger or complete the ritual. In preparation for exposures, the therapist and patient clarify what triggers, obsessional intrusions, and feared consequences the patient has in great detail. Generally, worksheets are utilized in the preliminary stages to detail and clarify these elements of their obsessions and responses to aid the therapy process. I highly recommend that therapists and patients use Jonathan S. Abramowitz's workbook *Getting Over OCD: A 10-Step Workbook for Taking Back Your Life*[10] or *The OCD Workbook: Your Guide to Breaking Free from Obsessive Compulsive Disorder*[11] by Bruce M. Hyman and Cherry Pedrick. Both workbooks are replete with the worksheets and other tools that will greatly aid the preparation and experience with ERP treatment protocols.

After clearly identifying one's obsessions, ERP practicing therapists will review the OCD patient's responses in order to successfully prevent their use. Responses to obsessions come in the form of avoidance behaviors and rituals. Because triggers lead to unpleasant anxiety, the patients learn to avoid things that could be triggering. For example, a person with contamination fears avoids certain places like public restrooms, trash cans, handrails, elevator buttons, and animals or people they fear are contaminated. For other subtypes of OCD, the patients will avoid items or situations relevant to those concerns. For the scrupulous, it is not uncommon for avoidance patterns to look like avoiding going to places of worship, avoiding religious items like scriptures or a cross, or avoiding anything they perceive as sinful (even if it is not a sin). For example, I had one patient who would avoid watching animated children's movies because inevitably the "prince" and "princess" (or similar character types) would kiss, and she feared that watching them kiss would arouse "lust" in her.

Another form of response is rituals. Rituals are the compulsive actions a person takes to try to neutralize the obsession. The OCD patient with contamination fears constantly washes their hands, the person with ordering or symmetry OCD is compulsively arranging items or counting them, and the person with the checking subtype of OCD is compulsively touching objects, engaging in special routines for reassurance (like flipping a light switch on and off a certain number of times), or asking others to check on something they've already checked. For Latter-day Saints with scrupulosity, the more common compulsive rituals include praying repetitively, confessing sins over and over, or searching the scriptures repeatedly to check about whether a behavior they did was a sin or not. Rituals are the classic compulsive behaviors most people commonly think of when they picture what OCD looks like.

There are other forms of rituals that are not as easy to identify as the major compulsive rituals. Called *mini-rituals*, any non-repetitive brief action used to "resist" the obsession could qualify. For example, holding your breath while in a room where you fear you might get contaminated or rubbing your hands on your clothes to get the "germs" off. These are closely associated with another category of rituals called *mental rituals* – rituals that are not performed outwardly. Mental rituals might include saying special words in your mind over and over, repeating lists, trying to analyze or parse through an unwanted obsession, or saying prayers mentally to one's self. Similarly, there are *reassurance-seeking rituals* whereby a person with OCD frequently engages in mental, verbal, or behavioral responses intended to reassure themselves. For example, a person may frequently take their temperature to make sure they are not falling ill, call friends to seek reassuring advice, or check with their bishop to see if something was a sin (or if it a sin that needs confession to a bishop). Whatever the category, all of these forms of responses are the compulsions that form the basis of OCD. They are temporary efforts to seek relief from anxiety that do not work in the long run, and in fact maintain and exacerbate the OCD experience for the sufferer. The goal of CBT and ERP treatment is *not* to help the person get rid of or fix their obsessions and anxieties, but rather to help the person be better at having these experiences.[12] In other words, ERP isn't intended to teach patients to resist or control their fears and anxieties, but to promote tolerance of those fears and anxieties so that patients can go forward and function better.[13] The goal is experiential learning through the exposure experiences.[14]

Utilizing the workbook(s) I suggested and completing the worksheets within them is important to the future steps of ERP treatment. Particularly, they will help identify the target symptoms and symptom severity as the therapist and patient create the exposure menu of triggers and obsessions, as well as the target rituals that will receive focus in exposure treatments.

Techniques in Exposure *and Response Prevention Treatment: Exposures*

Exposure and Response Prevention (ERP) utilizes two forms of exposures in treatment. The first is called *situational exposure* (or sometimes called *in vivo exposure*) and the latter is called *imaginal exposure*. The idea behind exposure coupled with response prevention is that the patient either mentally or physically exposes themselves to the very thing or things they fear. Then, when experiencing heightened anxiety, they commit to not responding the way they normally would (i.e. doing their compulsion). By experiencing the heightened anxiety from the exposure and feeling "triggered" and concomitantly refraining from responding compulsively, they are facing their fears and will eventually calm down. Over several experiences of being exposed without responding compulsively, the patient will develop what is called *habituation* – that is, they will become accustomed to the triggering exposure and realize it they can survive without engaging in the compulsion. When the patient is habituated to the exposure, the intensity of the anxiety will lessen due to repeated experiences with the triggering thought.

ERP sessions are generally longer than the standard therapy hour. Treatment generally requires 15 to 20 sessions of 90 minutes or longer (depending on if travel outside of an office is necessary to engage in a situational exposure). ERP treatment typically begins with a functional assessment to thoroughly understand the patient's idiosyncratic elements of their OCD. Cognitive therapy is frequently utilized to prepare the patient and challenge their maladaptive thinking patterns. Careful planning and identification of target triggers, obsessions, and compulsive responses (in order to prevent those responses from occurring and disrupting treatment) are reviewed. Coaching the patient not to ritualize or otherwise engage in responses is necessary, as well as issuing homework that challenges the patient to confront rather than avoid or ritualize.

Exposure and Response Prevention should usually begin under the guidance of a professional mental health provider but can eventually be self-practiced by the sufferer of OCD/scrupulosity.[15] That is because, to be done correctly, there are several necessary preliminary steps to enhance the effectiveness of the ERP. A competent counselor or therapist will spend time thoroughly understanding the patient's obsessions and compulsions.

Situational exposure begins by developing a list called an *exposure menu* that prioritizes the things that in the experience of the patient has triggered their obsessions. It usually includes 10 to 20 items placed in a hierarchy from things that are extremely anxiety provoking to moderately anxiety provoking down to those things that are mildly anxiety-provoking. To rate how anxiety-provoking an item is on the exposure menu, the patient and therapist use something called *Subjective Units of Distress* or SUDs scale on a scale from 0 to 100.

Exposure and Response Prevention should usually begin under the guidance of a professional mental health provider but can eventually be self-practiced by the sufferer of OCD/scrupulosity.[16] That is because, to be done correctly, there are several necessary preliminary steps to enhance the effectiveness of the ERP. A competent counselor or therapist will spend time thoroughly understanding the patient's obsessions and compulsions. For example, an OCD patient with fears of contamination that compulsively washes their hands excessively might list thoughts and behaviors that would cause them anxiety on a range like this:

100 – Rubbing their hands on a toilet seat in a public bathroom
95 – Crawling on the floor of a public bathroom
80 – Shaking hands with someone who is exiting a restroom
70 – Receiving cash from a store clerk who looks like they might have a cold
60 – Using an ATM machine without having on latex gloves
50 – Sitting in a seat in a car that your relative sat in while sick last week
40 – Being visited by someone who visited someone else last week in the hospital
30 – Parking their car next to a hospital or urgent care facility
20 – Loading their own dirty clothes into the washer
10 – Taking their own socks off at night

EXPOSURE AND RESPONSE Prevention treatment would then involve selecting a mid-range anxiety on the SUDS and engaging in that behavior to tolerate the obsessive thoughts without responding with their compulsion. So, in the case above, a person might sit in a seat they fear is contaminated because their relative sat in that seat a week ago while sick. The OCD patient would then sit in that seat exposing themselves to their obsessional fear but not engaging in washing their hands afterward. They would have to sit with their anxiety until they were habituated. Once they are able to tolerate that mid-range anxiety on their SUDS scale without responding compulsively on a consistent basis, they would try to expose themselves to something higher up on their exposure menu or "Fear Hierarchy" such as using an ATM machine bare handed or receiving cash from a store clerk (and not compulsively washing afterward). Once habituated at that level, they would continue to strive to address higher and higher issues on their Hierarchy. Patients should monitor their progress on forms provided by their therapist or in a self-help workbook.

Some patients choose to focus on an item on their exposure menu that is most impairing their functioning with a high SUDs level rather than starting at a mid-range level and working up their hierarchy. That's perfectly acceptable if the therapist deems the patient is motivated and prepared.

It is important that in preparing the exposure menu that a patient includes their worst fears. If they aren't including those items with the greatest feared consequences, they won't heal through ERP treatment. The exposures should be designed to contradict the patient's fear predictions. It is also important that the patient is very specific about the triggering items they will be exposed to and the proper corresponding level of anxiety as measured by SUDs levels. Finally, it is useful to get input from others. A patient may have one perspective, but the people they live with or who are close to them may have noticed certain avoidance patterns, rituals, mini-rituals, or reassurance-seeking rituals that the patient was less aware of or unaware of. Getting input from others can be important in creating a thorough and complete exposure menu.

If this sounds excruciatingly difficult for a person suffering with OCD, it absolutely is. It takes deep commitment to Response Prevention and often the patient needs help from a therapist and/or close relatives or friends in the form of a safety support individual or treatment buddy.[17] There are many possible pitfalls in the process. Some of the most common ones include: blocking, avoiding, numbing, or minimizing exposures; over reliance on safety signals with a spouse, friend, or other support; doing private mental rituals (such as counting or praying) to neutralize the exposure that would not be known by safety support individuals assisting the patient; or dissociating from the exposure experience due to the trauma of it.

Situational exposure requires that the exposure treatment be repeated often. During sessions, a patient may have practice sessions. For example, a patient with scrupulous obsessions whether or not it is a sin to have a statue of Jesus (because it might violate the second commandment of the ten commandments concerning not making any "graven image") might experience *in vivo* exposure with a statue of Jesus. The first time they do that exposure with the statue, their SUDs level may be as high as 80, but over an hour or so their SUDs level with the statue of Jesus may drop to a 40. A few days later in another treatment session, the patient might again undergo an exposure to a statue of Jesus, and their initial SUDs experience at the beginning of this second practice session may only rise to a 70 and then drop to a 30 by the end of the treatment session. On a third exposure, the initial level of anxiety might only reach a 50 in SUDs and drop to 10 by the end of the session. By the fourth exposure to the statue of Jesus, the initial level of anxiety may start at a 30 and drop to a 5 in their SUDs scale. It may take many sessions with many practices or exposures to have these types of decreases in SUDs scales, but it can be done. Additionally, in between sessions with their therapist, patients are expected to do "homework" whereby they continue their exposure work to support and reinforce their gains.

Using situational exposures for scrupulosity cases can be even more challenging. While some types of OCD have clear physical manifestations (like washing hands after fear of contamination), other forms of OCD and scrupulosity are more difficult to develop situational exposures for. Therefore, *imaginal exposures* offer the opportunity to address areas of concern that are not well suited for situational or *in vivo* exposures.

Let's be clear, no ethical therapist should ever ask a patient to "blatantly commit sins or violate religious commandments."[18] It just isn't ethical to ask a patient to go commit a sin (even a "small" or mental one) and then sit with it impenitently. Some intrusive, blasphemous thoughts should not be entertained (for example, some scrupulous patients have a mixture of erotic and sacred images). And clearly, any thoughts or actions that could be both sinful and violent should never be encouraged. Despite these challenges, imaginal exposures can be highly effective in working with scrupulosity patients. It is important to frame these imaginal exposure treatments as an effort to help the patient live their faith more freely. Dr. Abramowitz states that when working with scrupulous patients, he prepares them for imaginal exposures with the following discussion:

> "...with devoutly religious patients we discuss that although exposure might seem impious, its intent is to *strengthen one's faith* that God understands what's in the patient's heart… We often use the term *faith* rather than *uncertainty*, since religious patients can easily relate to the importance of a strong faith – which is indeed similar to learning to live with uncertainty…We find that the appeal to exposure as a means of strengthening one's religious faith often helps patients appreciate the goals of the technique and helps them engage in treatment even if it appears antithetical."[19]

Imaginal exposures are created in a similar fashion as situational exposures. The same care to include triggering items to target, careful consideration of the SUDs scale levels of anxiety, and inclusion of the most feared consequences should be included. An imaginal exposure menu is created and implemented just as in the case of situational exposures.

The benefit of imaginal exposures is that it allows the patient and therapist to explore thoughts and experiences that would be damaging and unethical in real life but can be acceptable to consider for the purposes of healing treatment. It allows the patient to experience the anxiety and habituate from those anxiety-provoking imaginal exposures without having to actually do something harmful or unethical. As one scholar and practitioner of ERP reminds us, "what's most important is that you (the patient) learn you can *have* obsessions, anxiety, and uncertainty without buying into them."[20]

Techniques in Exposure and Response Prevention Treatment: Response Prevention

Just as careful preparation is necessary for proper exposures, preparation is also needed to identify the response prevention components of ERP. Deciding on the target rituals that need to be stopped and any other compulsions or resistant or neutralizing responses is essential. To accomplish this, patients are asked to prepare a *response prevention plan* that describes the avoidance patterns, rituals, and behaviors that will be targeted. Identifying these compulsive behaviors is essential to ensure they are not utilized as a response to the exposures. Utilizing the suggested workbooks, patients fill out the Response Prevention Targets form[21] with a description of the rituals that won't be allowable as a response to the exposures.

For the scrupulous saint, response prevention plans will include the unique compulsive behaviors that they personally struggle with. Thus, for some, repetitive praying may be what they avoid if that is their typical compulsive behavior. For others, their response prevention might target repetitive confessions, mentally singing hymns to block out intrusive thoughts, or repeated questioning regarding the appropriateness or inappropriateness of a behavior within themselves or from others to quell their anxiety.

As patients consistently engage in situational and imaginal exposures and follow their response prevention plan with the guidance of their therapist (as well as complete their homework by themselves or with the support of their treatment buddy), ERP works for the majority of people suffering with OCD. It generally takes months of consistent effort, but the results are generally favorable. This is why ERP is an important component of treatment in the Saints Overcoming Scrupulosity model I suggest in this book.

Challenges with ERP and LDS Scrupulosity

What are some of the reasons ERP doesn't work for a few people? For ERP to work it has to be intentional, prolonged, and repeated and must cause some anxiety, some uncertainty, and test expectations.[22] Dr. Jonathan S. Abramowitz suggests that when people claim ERP doesn't work for them it most often is a result of a failure to meet these criteria. He responds to claims of ERP's failure for patients with the following statements:[23]

1. "Exposure won't be therapeutic if it is accidental."
2. "Exposure that is too quick won't give you a chance to learn what you need to do."
3. "One-time confrontation with a feared situation is not enough to get you over your obsession."
4. "For exposure to be helpful, you must 'go with' the anxious uncertain feelings when they occur.

Of course, there are times when the exposure menus or response prevention plans are poorly planned or executed. There are also times when a thorough understanding of the issues are not fully understood. When it comes to dealing with scrupulosity, one leading scholar[24] stresses the importance of the therapist being able to differentiate scrupulosity from normal religious practice by becoming knowledgeable about the beliefs, tenets, and practices of the patient's religion and demonstrate sensitivity to the client's religious values. Furthermore, therapists should "avoid intervention that could be construed as a direct threat to the client's personal religious beliefs or practices."[25]

Experiences show that sometimes many well-meaning non-LDS therapists who are treating LDS scrupulous sufferers do not fully understand LDS culture, practice, and theology. For example, the patient Lisa that was mentioned earlier in this book, was shown images of devils and scary iconography that represented fears of hell in her treatment by non-LDS therapists at a leading inpatient clinic in the Midwest of the United States. They failed to grasp how LDS doctrines about damnation differ from Catholic, Protestant, or other forms of Christianity. So, in developing her exposure menu, they did not really capture things she was actually afraid of, and it is possible she did not have the strength to advocate that the exposure menu be tailored to her unique concerns. LDS views about damnation or spiritual death have more to do with the relational loss of disconnection or separation from a loving Heavenly Father and/or loss of companionship with the Holy Ghost. That's not something that can be easily "exposed" to a scrupulous sufferer. In fact, many of the fears and obsessions about unworthiness, the nature of sin and righteousness, the roles of grace and works in salvation, the efficacy of prayer, and others are highly conceptual and don't readily translate into behavioral practices or exposures that can be contrived into exercises used in ERP.

Use of ERP with LDS cases of scrupulosity usually requires significant adaptations to accommodate the culture, practices, and theology of devout members of the Church.

Additional aspects of a CBT approach for treating OCD would also include exploration of various cognitive distortions,[26] such as catastrophizing, minimizing, personalizing, emotional reasoning, and others. Patients would be encouraged to engage in proactive behaviors such as exercise, social engagement, diaphragmatic breathing, grounding, and progressive muscle relaxation.

Summary

Exposure and Response Prevention (ERP) is a powerful tool in treating OCD. Saints struggling to overcome scrupulosity will likely benefit from engaging in ERP work with a competently trained therapist in the model. Therapists working with LDS patients with scrupulosity should be aware of the doctrines, practices, beliefs, customs, culture, and values of the faith, to tailor treatment to the unique needs of this population and enhance treatment effectiveness. Ideally, patients will have engaged in Phase I work, as well as the other cognitive therapy models suggested in Phase II of this book, in preparation for ERP treatment to enhance treatment effectiveness even further. Following ERP work, scrupulous saints should engage in Phase III work using Acceptance and Commitment Therapy (ACT) to further enhance treatment outcomes.

PHASE III: ACCEPTANCE AND COMMITMENT THERAPY (ACT)

TREATMENT FOR SCRUPULOSITY

*A*cceptance and Commitment Therapy (ACT[1*]) is another very effective treatment for OCD/scrupulosity. Even the leading proponent of ERP treatment for scrupulosity – Dr. Jonathan S. Abramowitz – now integrates ACT with ERP to enhance treatment efficacy into his practice and writings.[2] Originally developed by Dr. Stephen C. Hayes, who is a professor at the University of Nevada, Reno, ACT helps patients integrate aspects of cognitive and behavioral approaches in ways that promote greater psychological flexibility and firmer commitment towards acting on pre-determined values held by the patient.

Most patients with OCD want to fight off or eliminate the obsessive thoughts and feelings. ACT teaches them to accept that those feelings and thoughts will come and go, be mindful of their experience in the moment, take a more objective perspective of themselves, and then "move toward valued behavior"[3] despite the continued presence of the obsessive thoughts and feelings.

A basic description of the six core principles ACT commonly uses to help clients develop psychological flexibility include:

1. "Cognitive de-fusion: Learning methods to reduce the

tendency to reify thoughts, images, emotions, and memories.
2. Acceptance: Allowing thoughts to come and go without struggling with them.
3. Contact with the present moment: Awareness of the here and now, experienced with openness, interest, and receptiveness.
4. Observing the self: Accessing a transcendent sense of self, a continuity of consciousness which is unchanging.
5. Values: Discovering what is most important to oneself.
6. Committed action: Setting goals according to values and carrying them out responsibly."[4]

ACT therapists point out that most clients have a tendency towards fusion with their thoughts and actions. If people think about doing something bad, they sometimes feel as guilty as if they actually *did* that bad thing behaviorally. In terms of scrupulosity, this is called "Moral Thought-Action Fusion" or the "TAF Dilemma." Up to this point in the book, we've referred to this as one of the six maladaptive beliefs that fuel OCD – "importance of thought." In ACT, this concept is labeled "thought-action fusion" or TAF. While it is true that *intentional* unwholesome or impure thoughts could be the seeds of unrighteous behaviors (and can be a sin in their own right), there is still a great difference between a person having an impure thought and doing that impure act. Furthermore, an intrusive thought is not an intentional thought and should not be considered a sin. ACT therapists help clients defuse that TAF Dilemma in order to help them change towards valued actions the client has espoused.

ACT is an excellent approach to treating OCD because of the concept of *acceptance*. Counterintuitively, ACT helps the patient "lean in" to acceptance of the experience rather than resisting obsessive and intrusive thoughts with compulsions. One proponent of ACT quotes the famous psychologist Carl Jung's maxim, "What you resist persists."[5] ACT encourages the sufferer of scrupulosity to accept that the feelings and urges from obsessions will come and go in the patient's life, but they don't have to be resisted with compulsions or rituals. I once heard an ACT therapist, Annabella Hagen,[6] describe the concept of acceptance in ACT like a long stalk of seaweed or giant kelp that is rooted in the floor of the ocean but moves back and forth with the ebb and flow of the waves. The patient may have obsessional thoughts and feelings wash back and forth over them and not struggle against those obsessions, but take committed value-based actions irrespective of the obsessional thoughts. The patient can stay rooted to their values by taking committed action like the stalks of kelp are rooted to the ocean floor and not be harmed or damaged even though they are tossed by the waves. That metaphor has always struck me as an apt way of thinking about acceptance and mindfulness in treating scrupulosity. No sufferer of scrupulosity will be able to instantly shed themselves of obsessional thoughts and feelings – and fighting them often gives them more power. Both Dr. Schwartz's approach described previously and ACT require the person to refocus their efforts and actions toward something while continuing to feel the pressure of obsessional thoughts and feelings. Both Schwartz's model and ACT are mindfulness-based approaches that require the suspension of judgment or evaluation of a thought or urge until after the person has been able to take a more objective perspective. Mindfulness helps the obsessional thoughts and feelings subside on their own as the patient focuses on their own values and take committed actions based on those values. Mindfulness also helps the client to take perspective and stand back to view themselves in a transcendent context and make more proactive, rather than reactive, decisions. Just as many prophets have taught us to decide to keep the commandments long before the moment of temptation arises, the suffer of scrupulosity – in consultation with their priesthood leader and therapist – can predetermine what value-based actions the person should take when in the moment of obsessional thoughts and feelings. By not giving in to the compulsions and sticking by predetermined value-based actions that they've developed with trusted leaders and professionals, the sufferer of scrupulosity can hold onto their confidence when they follow the previously designed plan in the face of those moments of obsessional anguish.

One ACT therapist notes there are five stages of acceptance:[7]

1. *"Resisting*: struggling against what comes – 'Go away!'
2. *Exploring*: turning toward discomfort with curiosity – 'What am I feeling?'
3. *Tolerating:* safely enduring, holding steady – 'I don't like this, but I can stand it.'
4. *Allowing:* letting feelings come and go – 'It's okay, I can make space for this.'
5. *Befriending:* seeing value in difficult emotional experiences – 'What can I learn from this?'"

Learning to accept that intrusive thoughts and obsessions will enter and exit the life of a person with scrupulosity can be a growth step for the sufferer. Accepting that though the obsessions are challenging, the person does not have to become hooked by or stuck on these thoughts, but can choose how they will respond based on values they've predetermined. Defusing the thoughts from actions helps change the importance of thought component. "Thinking it does not make it so. Thinking it is not the same as acting on it," the patient may learn to say to themselves. Thus, the patient can begin to learn to differentiate a thought or feeling like fear from their actions and nullify the TAF dilemma.

Another therapist[8] using Acceptance and Commitment Therapy has described the difference between fear and acting with the acronyms FEAR and ACT:

- **Fusion** with your thoughts
- **Evaluation** of experience
- **Avoidance** of your experience
- **Reason-giving** for your behavior

Healthy alternative is to **ACT**:

- Accept your reactions and be present
- Choose a valued direction
- Take action

TAKING action is the commitment side of Acceptance and Commitment Therapy. Taking action toward a valued direction means being conscious and intentional in one's response. ERP focuses on response prevention. Similarly, ACT encourages the patient to not engage in their compulsive or ritualistic response, but goes a step further in predetermining a healthy response the patient can utilize instead, based on the values the therapist and patient have helped the patient to identify in their life.

In addition to my own research[9] on the usefulness of ACT with scrupulosity Dr. Michael P. Twohig, a Professor of Psychology and Utah State University (and former student of Dr. Stephen C. Hayes who developed ACT), has completed multiple studies[10] about the usefulness of ACT with OCD and scrupulosity. One of his studies[11] in particular examined scrupulosity with five LDS patients and found that utilizing ACT for eight sessions was a very effective treatment for Church members struggling with scrupulosity. Moreover, while the effectiveness of treatment remained high even at the 3-month follow up, there was very little negative effect of religious faith. One can only presume that because ACT encourages the patient to determine their values, the treatment is flexible for "faith-friendly" treatment of scrupulosity.

METAPHORS FROM ACT

With the ACT model, there are several metaphors that are commonly used in conjunction with ERP that aid the healing process. The following summary descriptions of the metaphors in this section of this chapter are drawn from writings of Dr. Jonathan S. Abramowitz as to how he uses ACT with ERP.[12]

- Tug-of-War
- Two Scales
- OCD Ditch
- OCD Quicksand
- Trudging through a Swamp
- Jerk at the Door
- Becoming the Chessboard
- Passengers on the Bus
- Leaves on a Stream

Tug of War

Imagine you get tricked into playing a game of tug-of-war with a con artist or monster. At first you start pulling, fearing they will drag you into a bottomless pit. When that doesn't seem to work, you try to pull harder and stronger. But that only seems to make it even worse because the game is rigged. It is not possible to win as long as you are pulling on the rope. The only way to "win" is to drop the rope and refuse to play.

In this analogy the monster or con artist is OCD. The tug one feels on the rope is one's obsessions. The efforts to pull back are the compulsions and rituals. "Winning" or overcoming OCD is found by letting go of the contest – to accept that the obsessions will continue to pull, but the choice the scrupulous saint has is to play a losing game by engaging in their compulsions or not play the game and moving on in a valued direction.

Two Scales

Consider your mind as if there were two scales. The first one measures how intrusive your thoughts are from 0-10. The second one measures how open and accepting you are of your intrusive thoughts from 0-10. Most people with OCD or scrupulosity can readily understand the first scale of intrusive thoughts intensity, but it is the second scale that influences the first one. When the openness scale is low, it locks the intrusive thoughts intensity scale at a higher level like a ratchet. But when the openness scale increases to a higher level, it frees the intrusiveness scale to fall to lower levels.

This metaphor helps the patient realize that regardless of how intense the intrusive thought is, that thought only has as much power as they allow it. If they fight the intrusive thought and resist it with intensity, the intrusive thought is reified as important and powerful. But if the patient accepts the thought coming and going in and out of their life (and their acceptance stems from them giving the thought no credence or value) and is open to letting it come and go without resisting it, then the thought lessens in intensity.

OCD Ditch

Pretend you are in a field wearing a blindfold with a bag of tools. You are left to wander the field blindfolded. Eventually, you fall into a ditch (everyone has distressing ditches in their life). Once in the ditch, you reach inside your tool bag and find a shovel. You begin to dig with your shovel, but after much exertion, you find that you are only deeper in your ditch. The way out is to *stop digging*.

OCD obsessions are like a ditch and compulsions are like the shovel. The patient uses the compulsions because they are the only tools the patient has or knows. Unfortunately, their compulsion tools only make the problem worse. To stop making the OCD worse, the patient needs to stop the compulsions and self-defeating rituals.

Notice how these first three metaphors – tug-of-war, two scales, and OCD ditch – all involve the paradox that the more the patient tries to solve their problem of obsessional intrusive thoughts with their only coping tool they have – compulsions – the worse it gets? That's the very nature of OCD – it is paradoxical. The more you try to solve it with compulsive rituals, the worse it gets. But the paradoxical nature of OCD also applies to avoidance behaviors, as well. The next couple of ACT metaphors illustrate the paradox issue between obsessions and avoidance behaviors.

OCD Quicksand

Getting stuck in quicksand is a dangerous proposition. Imagine you are hiking and you find yourself stuck in a pool of quicksand with no one to help you out. As you start to thrash around and struggle to run, you find yourself sinker deeper. The safer way to respond to quicksand is to lay flat and distribute your weight. It is counter-intuitive, but it what physics has taught us. By laying back like you are trying to float on your back, you will sink less and start to float more. Then you can slowly swim to safety using this smarter technique.

In the same way, when a patient starts to "sink" into obsessions, using compulsive rituals or avoidance patterns will paradoxically only make things worse. But choosing a smarter and wiser course of action based on values and knowledge of fundamental truths (like truths from physics or truths about mental health and the Gospel), there is more hope. This is what ACT therapists often mean when they describe "leaning in" to the OCD rather than resisting.

Trudging through a Swamp

Some have likened going through ERP to trudging through a swamp.[13] There's no way to go through a swamp without getting muddy, stinky, and filthy, but you can't get to the other side where the good things you want in life are waiting without going through the swamp. Going around the swamp is too far and impossible. If you want what is waiting for you on the other side, you have to go through the swamp.

This analogy supports the notion that treatment with ERP may be difficult, unpleasant, and painful, but there's a purpose to treatment – the "good things you want in life." Avoidance or compulsion will not get you those "good things," only treatment can accomplish that.

Learning to endure the difficulty of ERP without avoidance patterns or compulsive rituals will most likely lead to the peace the scrupulous saint hopes to find in their life.

Jerk at the Door

Suppose you are throwing a party at your new house and welcomed everyone on the street. You are enjoying getting to know your new neighbors. One of your neighbors that you've already had some unpleasant experiences with is walking up to your house. As you notice "the jerk" through the window, you think about rushing to the door and preventing him from entering the party, but that would ruin your chance to get to know everyone else if you are spending the whole party guarding the door. You could also let "the jerk" in but follow him around to ensure he doesn't do anything offensive, but that would again spoil the experience of the party for you. You realize the wisest course of action is to simply let him in, and go about enjoying your party without trying to control him. Learning to accept his presence and still act in ways that allow you to enjoy your other guests is your best option.

This analogy is useful for several situations for the scrupulous, but can be especially poignant in preparation for exposure treatments in ERP. Think of the jerk as the items on the exposure menu. They may be annoying and unpleasant, but you can habituate or learn to tolerate them and move forward enjoying your life.

Becoming the Chessboard

The game of chess has many components: the board, the pieces for the light or white team, and the pieces for the dark or black team. Imagine one of the teams represents the "OCD team" and the other the "Serenity team." When the "knight" of anxiety or the "rook" of obsession from the OCD team attacks a piece on the Serenity team, you might be tempted to want to run a valuable piece (for example, the Serenity team's queen) away from the attack or use it to fight off the attack, but remember what we've learned from all of the other analogies – the game is rigged and that avoidance or ritual response won't work. If you are playing the game, rooting for the Serenity team over the OCD team is like rooting for half of yourself to win and half of yourself to lose. Just as peace and serenity are part of you, so is anxiety.

All of the pieces on both teams are part of you and have their purposes. What if instead of picking sides you decided to become the chessboard? Think about it. The chessboard has a purpose to establish the rules, parameters, and boundaries of the game, but is a neutral observer to the game itself. By becoming the chessboard rather than picking one half of you to win and one half of you to lose, you step out of the rigged paradox. Becoming the chessboard if your best strategy and helps you "stand meta" to the OCD experience.

Passengers on the Bus

Suppose you are a bus driver driving your route. Passengers get on and get off in the normal course of events. But at one stop a rowdy bunch of unruly passengers get on the bus and start being obnoxious to you. They sit at the front of the bus and harangue you. They want you to drive them wherever they want – not the route you've planned. They threaten and cajole you. To appease them, you strike a deal with them that if they will sit in the back of the bus, you'll drive them wherever they want to go. This goes on for a while. Sometimes, they get loud and rowdy back there, but they leave you alone as long as you follow the route they tell you. Eventually, you grow tired of driving this bunch wherever they want to go. You want to drive where you desire. What if you didn't drive them where they want? They'd probably come back up front to try and intimidate you, but they probably wouldn't actually attack you. They might yell at you but not grab the wheel. You're in the driver's seat after all. In all honesty, they'd probably get tired of going where you are driving and would eventually get off.

In this metaphor the bus is your life. The passengers are your thoughts, but *you* are the driver of your life, not your thoughts. In imaginal exposures in ERP, the items on your imaginal exposure menu are like the rowdy bunch of passengers. You will have to deal with them for a while, but if you don't give in to them with compulsions (i.e. driving where they want you to go) you can still be in control of your life.

Leaves on a Stream

One final ACT metaphor is very useful for imaginal exposures to help patients "let go of… 'overattachment' to… obsessional thoughts and anxious feelings."[14] Imagine a stream flowing by in your mind with leaves floating along the surface. When an intrusive, obsessive thought enters your mind, place the thought on a leaf floating on the stream. Just watch and mindfully observe the thought on the leaf without trying to hurry it along or resist it. If it gets caught in an eddy, don't try to nudge it out into the moving flow – just watch and observe it. If other thoughts come along such as "This is scary" or "I don't like how that thought makes me feel" place those thoughts one by one on other leaves and watch them float by on the stream. If some thoughts come back and repeat, just allow them to float along on the stream as well. Don't try to control the thoughts or the stream – simply watch and stay in the moment as an observer from the shore.

This mindfulness metaphor helps scrupulous patients strengthen their "Impartial Spectator" that was discussed in Dr. Schwartz's model of Mindful CBT. Learning to stand more objectively and not try to control them, but simply be curious or aware of them helps to see the thoughts as just thoughts and leads to de-fusion of the thought-action fusion (TAF) dilemma.

Summary of ACT Treatment

Acceptance and Commitment Therapy (ACT) has become a powerful integration with ERP treatment to enhance efficacy. The focus on mindfully accepting the ingress and egress of obsessional thoughts without resistance allows the sufferer of OCD to devalue the thoughts and move forward with predetermined committed actions based on their values. It has become a powerful contribution in my treatment experiences.

Moving forward in this chapter, I will first summarize the SOS model which typically leads to successful treatment outcomes for patients. But there are cases where second-line treatments may be required. This chapter will conclude with brief descriptions of Dialectical Behavior Therapy (DBT) and Eye Movement Desensitization and Reprocessing (EMDR) where such treatment option may be necessary.

Summary of the "Saints Overcoming Scrupulosity" Treatment Approach

Typically, when I work with patients diagnosed with scrupulosity, I will follow the following protocol:

1. Joining/Building a Relationship of Trust
2. Assessment (Typically, the Penn Inventory of Scrupulosity or PIOS, but I may use other diagnostic assessment tools if I deem it reasonable – for example the Beck Depression Inventory or Beck Anxiety Inventory if the client presents with these symptoms as well)
3. Ecclesiastical Consultation (If possible – clients must sign as Release of Information form if they choose for me to work with the priesthood leader, but it always their choice)
4. Client's Acceptance of Diagnosis and the Development of a Treatment Plan
5. Medication Evaluation Referral to a Competent Medical Doctor
6. Phase I – Foundational Truths (Spiritual discussions and reframes about foundational doctrinal truths as outlined in this book and as they are relevant to the client's concerns and the six maladaptive beliefs that fuel OCD; also, God-

attachment work, family of origin work, adaptive and maladaptive perfectionism, stages of faith model and its potential role in their development of the scrupulosity subtype, and self-compassion as they pertain to the six maladaptive beliefs.)
7. Phase II – CBT: Strategic Paradoxes, Schwartz and the Four R's, MBCT, and ERP
8. Phase III – Acceptance and Commitment Therapy (ACT)

TYPICALLY, clients make excellent progress after completing all three phases of treatment. There are times however, when a patient needs more help than what has been provided. In therapy we call this a "second line" of treatment. When the front line of treatment (in this case Phases 1-3) does not lead to adequate progress, clients may benefit from a second line of treatment approaches. Because I am not certified in these therapy approaches, I always refer patients needing these approaches out to other professionals who are so certified. These other approaches are Dialectical Behavior Therapy (DBT) and Eye Movement Desensitization and Reprocessing (EMDR).

DIALECTICAL BEHAVIOR THERAPY

Dialectical Behavior Therapy (DBT) was developed by Dr. Marsha M. Linehan, Professor Emeritus at the University of Washington. Her work was originally designed for treating suicidal and parasuicidal women and those diagnosed with Borderline Personality Disorder. In addition to Borderline Personality Disorder, this evidenced-based practice has also been successful in the treatment of mood disorders, substance abuse, post-traumatic stress disorder (PTSD), and traumatic brain injuries. Recently, DBT has been tried and shows some promise with sexual abuse and non-suicidal self-injurious behaviors. While no known rigorous studies of DBT usage with scrupulosity are known at this date, anecdotally clinicians have begun trying DBT with OCD with descriptions of results on a case by case basis.

DBT is a type of cognitive-behavioral therapy (CBT) that incorporates elements of acceptance and mindfulness. Like ACT and Schwartz's Mindfulness-based CBT (the Four Step regimen), DBT seeks to help the patient use mindfulness, acceptance, and focusing on alternative activities despite experiencing unwanted thoughts and feelings. The term "dialectical" means a "synthesis or integration of opposites"[15] When I try to explain dialecticism to my students, I use coins as an example and compare dualism to dialecticism. Dualism would be comparing two different coins (for example, a nickel vs. a quarter), but dialecticism is seeing how both the heads and the tails are part of the same coin. That is, there are two opposing sides to the quarter (heads and tails) but both heads and tails are integrated or synthesized into the same coin.

A person with Borderline Personality Disorder (BPD) has a hard time seeing that good and bad can be in the same person. They tend to think dualistically and will put a person on a high pedestal if they think they are good. They will see the person as "all good" until that person does something wrong (it could even be a very small imperfection) and then they will see the person as "all bad" in a concept psychological theory calls "splitting." Because of their dualistic thinking, the person with BPD cannot accept even small elements of bad in a good person or small elements of good in a bad person. It's all or nothing thinking in dualism. But dialectical thinking looks for how opposites (like good and bad) can be integrated into one thing or being. Thus, when we learn to think about others dialectically, we can still see the good in them despite their imperfections or weaknesses. Learning to think dialectically about themselves could be a very beneficial cognitive skill for people with scrupulosity who need to gain greater psychological flexibility and reduce their rigidity about how they view themselves. Through a combination of individual therapy, group therapy, therapist team consultation, and phone coaching, DBT works to address four key skill sets:

- Distress tolerance – learning to distract or soothe one's self when facing unpleasant or disturbing thoughts and feelings; the ability to tolerate or refocus on something else while the unpleasant thoughts and emotions remain
- Emotional Regulation – learning to manage or control one's feelings, realizing that one's powerful emotions will change/lessen over time (especially for OCD – when one does not give in to acting compulsively)
- Interpersonal effectiveness – learning mange your feelings in social interactions so that one can maintain effective, healthy relationships with others
- Mindfulness – learning to redirect your thoughts toward the present moment in a non-judgmental way.

If a patient has tried the front-line treatments that I suggest (Phases 1-3, including ERP and ACT), and still is having significant distress from scrupulosity, DBT may be the next step for them.

Trauma and EMDR

Because some people struggling with scrupulosity may have also experienced significant traumas in their life, it may be necessary to address those traumas which may be compounding or exacerbating their scrupulosity. Some may even argue that living with scrupulosity can be traumatizing, but there may also be other traumas such as childhood abuse, witnessing accidents or violence, significant losses that may be sudden and unexpected, or much, much more. Unfortunately, mortality allots a seemingly unending supply of potential traumas in life that we may experience. Often these traumas can compound upon one another and/or upon mental illnesses. Dealing with trauma is an essential part of all therapies to some extent, but one model is very direct and effective at specifically addressing trauma – Eye Movement Desensitization and Reprocessing (EMDR). EMDR was developed by Dr. Francine Shapiro in the late 1980's and 1990's. It involves bilateral eye movements (usually by focusing on a wand or light moving laterally back and forth controlled by the therapist) while recalling negative, traumatic feelings, memories, and images. Interestingly, by stimulating both sides of the brain through bilateral eye movements while recalling traumatic feelings and images, the patient's brain begins to heal and the feelings (including physical arousal and/or hypervigilance) become desensitized or lessened. What used to take many years of processing, can be relieved in a much shorter time frame.

I was initially very skeptical of EMDR when I first heard of it in the mid-1990's. It seemed completely counter to what I was learning about traditional "talk therapy." But the scientific research that has accumulated over the decades has changed my opinion of the matter. Study after study has demonstrated the effectiveness of EMDR with trauma, so I now choose to refer to a colleague in our office that is certified in EMDR when I have cases with severe trauma. Having watched her work with my patients for the first half of a session and then taking over the verbal processing in the latter half of the session, I am appreciative of the tremendous healing that EMDR has to offer. For scrupulosity patients who also have significant traumatic events to address, EMDR may be warranted.

WORKING as a Team with Specialists

As you may have gathered by now in this chapter, no "one-size-fits-all" approach is totally effective for treating scrupulosity. This is why I have a three-phase approach in my model that integrates the foundational truths of our faith with effective treatments (CBT – including ERP – and ACT) that have scholarly studies supporting their effectiveness in treating scrupulosity. Additionally, I refer out to specialists if geography or a need for second line treatments are warranted. As mentioned earlier, I always want patients to begin the therapy process by having a thorough physical by a competent medical doctor and have a psychiatrist (if possible) prescribe appropriate medications. Without such coordinated co-consultation, therapy effectiveness will be reduced. Any therapist desiring to treat scrupulosity should take this "team of specialists" approach if they want to truly help their patients get the coordinated care that is needed to effectively address the mental health aspects of scrupulosity.

In the next chapter, we will address the other key "specialist" a therapist should coordinate the patient's care with if they truly want to help any Latter-day Saint struggling with scrupulosity – the priesthood leader (usually bishop, branch president, or stake president). Coordinating with the patient's priesthood leader is crucial (when possible), and greatly adds to the chances of successful treatment when treating scrupulosity.

WHAT EVERY BISHOP OR PRESIDENT OUGHT TO KNOW ABOUT SCRUPULOSITY: CONSULTING WITH PRIESTHOOD LEADERS

The calling of a bishop or branch president may be one of the most difficult and rewarding experiences in the Church. Having served as a bishop, I know what it is like to be on the front lines of caring for, ministering to, and counseling with the members of my ward through very difficult, sweet, and poignant moments of their lives. Like most released bishops, I have very tender feelings about my experience serving as a bishop which lends to my great respect to those who currently serve in that sacred office throughout the world. In this chapter I outline a few things I believe would benefit other bishops and keyholding priesthood leaders (such as branch presidents, district presidents, stake presidents, and mission presidents).

THE TRAINING of a Bishop or Other Keyholding Priesthood Leader

Most keyholders in the Church who are in a position to counsel with the Saints, hear confessions, deal with financial matters, and assist members who are struggling with mental health concerns are not trained for addressing mental health matters like OCD/scrupulosity. It is true that they are well trained by their experiences in the

Church, previous callings, and incredible faith in the Lord to be great leaders in the Lord's Church, but the Church offers no formal coursework or degrees in counseling to all of the Judges in Israel. They rely wholly on the gifts of the Spirit, their file leaders in the Priesthood above them, and some handbook guidance available to them. Most often they do a remarkable job. For example, when I was a young father, I once had a bishop who was an accountant give me some of the best parenting advice about attachment regarding one of my adopted children, and I knew that it was the Lord speaking to me through His servant despite the fact that his education was in business rather than family therapy. I know the Lord helps these good brethren to counsel with the Saints beyond their mere mortal capacities, knowledge, and experience.

But almost every bishop, branch president, and stake president I have ever met is eager to learn more for themselves how to be better at counseling with their ward or stake members. They often consult with therapists they trust either in private practice or through LDS Family Services on issues they are addressing. This chapter is meant to be one more aid on top of their existing capacities and Heaven-inspired revelation in working with members of the Church who struggle with OCD/scrupulosity. Though this book is not sufficient training for a priesthood leader to conduct therapy or pastoral counseling to the point of completely healing the scrupulous, it can be a first step for recognizing, understanding, and referring to a therapist when a scrupulous ward member needs help.

Key Holders **and the Gift of Discernment**

Key holders with the gift of discernment must discern between sin and mental health issues. Thus, priesthood leaders who hold the keys of discernment must rely on the Holy Ghost to help them ascertain the entanglements of sin and scrupulosity, and must decide by that same Spirit what mitigating factors (if any) exist in a case they are adjudicating. The reminder about what the Savior means by "judging" as a means of delivering, saving, advocating for, and redeeming as

Christ did (as described earlier in this book) is always warranted in such deliberations. In my experience as both a therapist and a previous bishop, here are some common signs that the situation probably involves scrupulosity, rather than sin:

- Member describes intrusive thoughts they cannot get rid of (could be blasphemous, sexual, or both)
- Member seems "overly concerned" about minuscule details about sin, repentance, and moral quandaries
- Member confesses same sins over and over (or adds minute, perhaps irrelevant details as addendums)
- Member prays repetitively in a manner that gets in the way of daily functioning
- Member seems over-reliant on the priesthood leader's opinion to the point where they repeatedly don't trust their own perspective (which robs them of their spiritual growth, self-reliance, and maturity)
- Member repeatedly seeks counseling or advise because they are "not sure if something is a sin"
- Member obsesses about details of repentance that they cannot easily do or ascertain (for example, not sure how or if restitution is possible or sufficient; or worries their confession was not complete enough)
- Member still feels unforgiven despite repeated assurances from priesthood leaders that their repentance is sufficient

OF COURSE, there may be other signs or features of scrupulosity a member may present with not on the list above. Often there are idiosyncratic or unique presentations of scrupulosity never before demonstrated (for example, the case of Craig[1*] who got headaches until he confessed to his bishop is somewhat atypical). The key is to recognize when a member is using an element of our religion compulsively to try to neutralize or quiet an obsession. Feelings like guilt could be a legitimate response to sinful behavior, but they could also be an obsessional feeling that won't go away even though it is not based on any sinful behavior. The priesthood leader must use the gift of discernment to try to ferret out the difference. To aid the priesthood leader in differentiating between legitimate guilt and obsessional guilt the general rule is: when in doubt, pray and ask for help. Ask God for revelation, but also don't hesitate to consult with a competent therapist with some experience with scrupulosity. Co-consultation with a therapist (even if confidential information like names are never disclosed) is always welcome. In general, it is advisable for priesthood leaders to seek out competent therapists (preferably members of the Church or therapists familiar with our Church's beliefs and teachings if available) that they can turn to, ask questions of, or refer to when they start their ministry in their new calling. Having clinicians that they can trust will make working with Church members with mental health concerns much easier for the priesthood leader.

THE TEN COMMANDMENTS FOR the Scrupulous

Seeking help from those with experience with scrupulosity might also include some interfaith dialogue about the subject. For example, our Catholic clergy friends have many centuries of experience dealing with the scrupulous and confession. It would be wise for us to glean some counsel from their wisdom and adapt it to fit our own situation. The first book that I ever read about scrupulosity was from a former Catholic priest and Professor of Pastoral Counseling at Loyola University Maryland, Dr. Joseph W. Ciarrocchi, entitled *The Doubting Disease: Help for Scrupulosity and Religious Compulsions.*[2] Dr. Ciarrocchi's book is an oft-cited resource for understanding cognitive-behavioral approaches to treating scrupulosity. He defined scrupulosity as "seeing sin where there is none." Another important and prolific writer in the subject of scrupulosity is Father Thomas M. Santa, CSsR, a Catholic priest that has over twenty years of experience ministering to and working with scrupulosity among

members of his faith. He published the key book *Understanding Scrupulosity*[3] as well as many other resources for those struggling with this illness. One of his available publications on the internet is made available by Scrupulous Anonymous and is entitled the "Ten Commandments for the Scrupulous."[4] The following is an adaptation for Latter-day Saints which is a composite of my own wording and language developed by the patient Craig, described earlier in this chapter.

<u>Ten Commandments for the Scrupulous (Adapted for Latter-day Saints)</u>

1. Do not repeat a confession of sin when it has been told to the proper priesthood authority in a previous confession even if you doubt it was told, or doubt it was told in a sufficiently adequate and complete way.
2. Do not confess doubtful sins; rather, only confess sins that are clear and certain.
3. Once you have repented before the Lord (as measured by your priesthood leader stating your repentance has been sufficient), do not seek additional forgiveness for the same sins – for any reason.
4. Do not worry about accidentally breaking your fast on Fast Sunday unless you consciously put food and drink in your mouth as a meal.
5. Do not worry about powerful and vivid thoughts, desires, feelings, emotional outbursts, impulses, or imaginings involving sex and religion that intrude on your mind unless you deliberately generate them for the purpose of offending God.
6. Do not engage in repetitive religious rituals (such as repetitive prayer or praying until you get it "just right") that impede daily functioning. Trust that "vain repetitions" are not necessary for salvation and only impair mental health.
7. You shall trust your priesthood leader's counsel regarding repentance and not repeat confessions made either to your

current or previous priesthood leaders or re-repent of your previous sins.
8. When you experience doubt and fears, you will view that doubt and fear as evidence that the thoughts and feelings are *not* from the Holy Ghost. Trust that God will *not* communicate to the scrupulous through doubt and fear, but rather through clear encouragement that promotes faith and understanding.
9. When you are doubtful or uncertain about actions you should or should not take, trust that using your conscience and the Light of Christ and/or the Gift of the Holy Ghost will guide you in a way that you do not have to fear sin, if you sincerely do whatever you decide is the right thing.
10. You shall put your total faith in the Atonement of Jesus Christ, trusting in His grace and mercy, and know that God loves you and will never allow you to inadvertently lose your soul. (To lose one's soul one must persistently use their moral agency to consciously, purposefully, willfully, and determinedly choose a life of sin and disbelief. God will always stretch forth His hand to strive to reclaim the sinner, and there are no loopholes to trap a soul). Believe that God's orientation is to love, succor, advocate for, save, forgive, aid, deliver, and redeem you.

My patient Craig also added two important reminders as addendums that gave additional help to him, which I highly recommend and endorse:

- Remember: Feelings, impulses, and ideas are neither acts of the will nor accomplished facts.
- Remember: Temptations are not sins. Even Jesus was tempted by the Devil and never sinned.

Priesthood leaders who give such principles to ward members suffering with scrupulosity will help them have a starting block to build confidence and assurance. The scrupulous need to begin with such firm declarations to begin combating the obsessions without yielding to their compulsions. Understand that every time a member comes in a re-confesses something for the umpteenth time, they are engaging in a compulsion that only reinforces their obsessions thereby allowing those obsessions to grow and grow. Priesthood leaders must lovingly, but clearly, give firm guidelines about what is and is not the type of sins that need confessing and then hold the member to those guidelines. Priesthood leaders may wish to set guidelines or schedules to help the person who prays repetitively and uses prayer as a compulsion, to develop a greater balance between fervent prayer and daily activity. They should also refer the member to a competent therapist and seek to engage in lawful co-consultation with the therapist. While the bishop is entitled to engage in pastoral counseling (and should understand that is the role they are engaging in), they should also recognize the limits of their scope of competence or training and work with therapists or other clinicians in a team approach.

Scrupulosity is More Than Just a Confidence or Self-Worth Issue

I hope bishops and other priesthood leaders recognize that scrupulosity is more than just an issue of lacking confidence and low self-worth. While scrupulosity saps both self-confidence and self-worth, it is so much more. Low self-worth and lacking confidence are symptoms, not the root cause, among the scrupulous members, and there may also be many members of their ward, branch, district, or stake that have low self-worth, lack confidence, and struggle with perfectionism that are not suffering from scrupulosity. Scrupulosity is a medical condition in the brain that affects the mental health of the sufferer. It is OCD, but a type of OCD that insidiously infects the very faith that ought to be a source of comfort and strength in fighting this affliction and infirmity in their life. While priesthood leaders may wish to address the issues of low self-worth and poor confidence, they must also seek to connect the member with competent mental health providers to treat the condition.

I love a talk in the January 2005 *Ensign* magazine by Elder Glenn L. Pace entitled "Confidence and Self-Worth."[5] I often have patients read that talk as a recommended resource. The talk discusses being too "preoccupied with our weaknesses," teaches that in the premortal life we walked and talked with God and Christ and "basked in the light of the presence of God and enjoyed His smiles," and that the mission and purpose of the Gospel is to foster and develop our eternal growth to "make us like our Heavenly Parent."[6] Thus, Elder Pace's article highlights many of the solutions to the symptoms of low self-worth and a lack of confidence that (in the case of scrupulosity) are resulting symptoms of the deeper issue of scrupulosity. But scrupulosity is the underlying cause of those symptoms of lack of confidence and low self-worth, not the other way around. At a deeper level than lacking confidence and low self-worth, scrupulosity is fundamentally a malfunction in how a brain processes thoughts and feelings that results in OCD with the manner or variant of that OCD being religiously-oriented obsessions and compulsions. It needs therapeutic (and possibly medical) treatment – not simply a pep talk or blessing alone (as wonderful as those things are).

MENTAL ILLNESS MAY BE a Mitigating Factor to Consider in Church Disciplinary Councils

At times, scrupulosity and other mental health issues, may be a mitigating factor in Church disciplinary councils. The member may even be making false confessions of sins they aren't even sure they committed to "cover their bases" because they want to be penitent of things they "might have done" but have little to no certainty whether or not they've committed those sins. There is a rare, but legitimate, form of OCD called "false memory" OCD whereby an intrusive thought about an act comes into the patient's mind over and over and over again until the patient believes they might have actually done the sinful thing that has been in their mind so long. The persistence of the intrusive obsessive thought creates such a vividness of the act that they begin to believe that they might have actually done the sinful thing that has been running in their mind over and over and over again. This "false memory" OCD is somewhat similar to something called HOCD (or OCD with a subtype regarding sexual orientation)[7] where the person is so frightened or concerned that they might be homosexual (even though they are not) because they have persistent, intrusive, and obsessional thoughts or fears about them possibly being homosexual that they even begin to question their sexual orientation despite having no attraction to people of the same sex. Understand that repetitive, persistent, and unrelenting obsessional thoughts can cause a person with OCD to really start to lose touch with basic truths about themselves. They can lose their sense of perspective entirely to these powerful obsessional thoughts, impulses, and feelings.

Scrupulous Members May Say Their Therapist Told Them to Do "Weird" Stuff

Always vet the therapist before referring (because unfortunately there is a very wide range of competence among therapists and counselors), but realize that with some of these treatments, members may misinterpret what the therapist advised. If a Release of Information (ROI) form has been signed by the client allowing therapists and ecclesiastical leaders to co-consult, take advantage of that important opportunity to be sure the two of you are on the same page. A therapist may have a strategic reason for saying something that doesn't sound just right, or the client may not have interpreted what the therapist said correctly.

Some things a therapist asks a patient to do will definitely sound weird. For example, in using Exposure and Response Prevention (ERP) the therapist will be seeking to have the patient do things that are on their exposure menu list (like watch a television show on the sabbath, if that's something a patient believes might be sinful, but is not necessarily so) and then not engage in their compulsion (praying or confessing). Realize competent therapists are not going to encourage a person to commit actual sins, but they may ask a patient to do an activity or behavior that the *patient* erroneously thinks is a sin[8*] and then use that as a means to accomplish response prevention of the compulsions.

When a priesthood leader hears things that don't sound right to them, they should contact the therapist. If the therapist is legally allowed to co-consult with a Release of Information form in place, competent therapists will welcome the opportunity to describe the treatment process with the priesthood leader. It is always important for the therapist and priesthood leader to communicate where possible and support one another's efforts as they work with the scrupulous member.

Most Members Suffering from Scrupulosity are Already "Worthy"

In counseling with members who have scrupulosity, priesthood leaders will likely be guided by the Spirit that the member in question is most likely already worthy and forgiven of any sins in the eyes of God. Very often the member in question has not learned that there is a distinct difference between sins, afflictions, errors, imperfections, and weaknesses. The Lord made it very clear that He sees a distinction between errors or mistakes, imperfections due to a lack of knowledge, and sins (Doctrine and Covenants 1:24-28). Recently, Tad R. Callister pointed out that the Atonement of Jesus Christ not only covers physical death through the resurrection, and spiritual death (sin) through repentance and obedience to the laws and ordinances of the Gospel, but also overcomes two other categories he labels "afflictions and infirmities 'of every kind' (Alma 7:11)" and "human weaknesses and imperfections that prevent us from becoming more like God."[9] Scrupulosity is an "infirmity" – a mental illness – not a sin. While some members of the Church with scrupulosity will sin from time to time and need to repent (as we all do), more often they are struggling because they conflate the category of infirmity (scrupulosity) or human weaknesses and imperfections with the category of sin which leads to spiritual death. Their anxiety at having an imperfection or weakness is erroneously intertwined with impending spiritual death due to sin. That may be why they often sound dire and extreme in their confessions to priesthood leaders.

Priesthood leaders with the keys of discernment must gently, but very clearly help the member distinguish between sin, illness (scrupulosity), and human imperfection or weakness. They also must assure them that the Atonement of Jesus Christ is fully encompassing of all of these categories (physical death, sin or spiritual death, afflictions and infirmities, and human weaknesses and imperfections). Priesthood leaders should emphasize greater faith in the mercy and grace of the Atonement of Jesus Christ for these members suffering with scrupulosity. If a priesthood leader discerns by the Spirit that the Lord has forgiven the scrupulous member of any sins he or she has confessed and repented of, he should make that statement clearly to the member and then have the member read this quote from Elder Richard G. Scott's General Conference talk "Peace of Conscience and Peace of Mind":

> "Now if you are one who cannot forgive yourself for serious past transgressions—even when a judge in Israel has assured that you have properly repented—if you feel compelled to continually condemn yourself and suffer by frequently recalling the details of past errors, I plead with all of my soul that you ponder this statement of the Savior:
>
> "He who has repented of his sins, the same is forgiven, and I, the Lord, remember them no more.
>
> "By this ye may know if a man repenteth of his sins— ... he will confess them and forsake them."
>
> "To continue to suffer when there has been proper repentance is not prompted by the Savior but the master of deceit, whose goal is to bind and enslave you. Satan will press you to continue to relive the details of past mistakes, knowing that such thoughts make forgiveness seem

unattainable. In this way Satan attempts to tie strings to the mind and body so that he can manipulate you like a puppet.

"I testify that when a bishop or stake president has confirmed that your repentance is sufficient, know that your obedience has allowed the Atonement of Jesus Christ to satisfy the demands of justice for the laws you have broken. Therefore, you are now free. Please believe it. To continually suffer the distressing effects of sin after adequate repentance, while not intended, is to deny the efficacy of the Savior's Atonement in your behalf."[10]

As I counseled with ward members while serving as a bishop (and at other times as a therapist), I would often counsel them to speak to the Lord and ask for Him to be clear in His communication to them. I would tell them that God does not speak to us in doubt. I would encourage them to pray and ask God to bless them so that if they really commit a sin that needs repenting that He will make it clear to them in unmistakable, non-doubtful ways. That way if they are stuck in a doubt, they can know it is their scrupulosity, not from God. But if it is from the Spirit, He will make their need to repent clear and unmistakable to them. I would encourage them to pray for the gift of discernment and then hone their ability to discern between the Holy Ghost and scrupulosity (as well as discerning between mind, heart, and spirit – see Doctrine and Covenants 8:2-3) through practice.

Priesthood leaders need to be loving, but clear in spelling out what types of things they want the member to come to them to confess, what things they can prayerfully repent of on their own between the member and the Lord, and what things are not sins but are simply human error where the Atonement still applies in their lives. Loving, but clear guidelines can go a long way in helping the member to develop the spiritual self-reliance they need to overcome scrupulosity.

TO THE SCRUPULOUS SAINT

*I*n this book, I have addressed priesthood leaders, practitioners, and patients, but this concluding chapter is directed to those patients – the scrupulous saints – who are reading this book. It is my deepest hope that those reading this book will feel encouraged and hopeful that healing from scrupulosity is possible. Often this requires a cognitive paradigm shift or change in perspective. It requires you to see the feelings, urges, and obsessions you experience as a mental health issue, not a spiritual deficiency. That new perspective can be freeing and uplifting.

Let me illustrate what I mean by a "change in perspective" with a story. Years ago, when my family and I lived in Illinois, I was flying out of St. Louis on a cold, rainy day to go present at a conference. The sky was heavy and dark with clouds. It was thoroughly depressing, miserable weather. I worried the planes wouldn't be allowed to take off in the storm. But to my surprise, we were allowed to take off and soon we were flying high above the clouds enjoying the brilliant sunlight. It metaphorically reminded me that God's love or influence is always there, but it is sometimes blocked out by our mortal experiences in the same way that the sun had been there all along above the clouds. In those moments, we have to trust He is there loving us, even if we can't feel Him. Scrupulosity is an anxiety disorder that, like the clouds, sometimes dims our perspectives and emotions. Yet, when we can climb to a new vantage point, we can see the clouds of scrupulosity below us and feel the effects of a loving Father in Heaven blessing us. Therapy that changes our perspective cognitively, emotionally, and experientially is how we climb to new vantage points – and that makes all the difference.

This book asks you, the scrupulous saint, to change your plea to heaven from "Save Our Souls" to "Saints Overcoming Scrupulosity" – a shift from perceiving your experiences with doubt, despair, and debilitating obsessions and compulsions as a sin or spiritual deficit to seeing them for what they truly are as impulses in your brain stemming from OCD. This newfound perspective can give you a solid foundation of truth upon which you can build, and "truth shall make you free" (John 8:32).

Working in Phase I of the Saints Overcoming Scrupulosity (SOS) model emphasizes both mental health and Gospel truths to reframe your perspectives about mental illness, God, your experiences growing up, your attachment and family of origin experiences, your understanding of healthy forms of perfectionism vs. unhealthy maladaptive perfectionism, self-compassion, and much, much more. It is designed to help you use faith to increase your tolerance for uncertainty, help you see perfectionism from a growth mindset, and help you address the other maladaptive beliefs that fuel OCD.

Phase II focuses on various CBT models based with mindfulness components and especially assist you through the difficult, but necessary elements of Exposure and Response Prevention (ERP) treatments. Using the gold-standard treatment approach of ERP will especially help you overcome scrupulosity when it is properly tailored to your unique experiences and beliefs as a Latter-day Saint.

Phase III furthers the healing process through Acceptance and Commitment Therapy (ACT). In this phase you will learn to accept rather than resist the thoughts, urges, and impulses because you can defuse or distinguish your thoughts from actions and devalue the thoughts. By according the thoughts less importance, you give them less power over your life. You can move forward in life based on a course of action predetermined by the values *you* establish for your life, not the values the mental illness of OCD tries to set for you.

I hope that this book will prompt you to seek help from a competent mental health professional such as a therapist, counselor, psychologist, social worker, and/or a psychiatrist who specializes in treating OCD and scrupulosity. No competent mental health professional will desire to do anything that will compromise your religious standards or beliefs. Good mental health professionals are trained to have respect for people's cultures, religions, and values as a core fundamental of good ethical practice. They will be there to help you. Hopefully, your priesthood leader will have found competent therapists and counselors that he trusts and can refer you to, if you do not have an idea where to start.

Know that God loves you and His orientation is to bless you, not condemn you. Through changing your perspectives and working with your therapist, you will be able to enjoy living the Gospel in a much healthier way. There is hope for you to overcome scrupulosity as others have. May you find the support you need to be among the many saints overcoming scrupulosity and feel the peace God intends for you to find in your life.

APPENDIX – RESOURCES FOR MINDFUL SELF-COMPASSION

Books:

Neff, Kristen (2011). *Self-Compassion: The Proven Power of Being Kind to Yourself*, New York, NY: William Morrow, an imprint of HarperCollins.

McGonigal, Kelly (2016). *The Science of Compassion: A Modern Approach for Cultivating Empathy, Love, and Connection.* (Audiobook). Louisville, CO: Sounds True Publishing.

Harris, Russ. (2019). *ACT Made Simple: An Easy-to-Read Primer on Acceptance and Commitment Therapy.* Oakland, CA: New Harbinger Publications, Inc.

Neff, Kristen and Germer, Chris (2018). The Mindful Self-Compassion Workbook: A Proven Way to Accept Yourself, Build Inner Strength, and Thrive. New York, NY: Guilford Press.

Apps for Smart Phones:

There are numerous apps – too numerous to list all here – for Smart Phones that are popular. Some (like the Calm app) are popular but have subscription fees. Others (like Mindfulness Coach – published by the U.S. Department of Veterans Affairs) are completely free. Consumers should always be careful to check for pricing of apps (including added on internal subscriptions) before selecting an app that is right for them.

Websites:
   https://chrisgermer.com

Dr. Chris Germer is a leading expert, along with Dr. Kristen Neff, in mindful self-compassion (MSC). On his website he has multiple free "Audio Meditations" that are downloadable for one's use. Dr. Germer leads the listener through various excellent meditations that exemplify MSC.

ABOUT THE AUTHOR

Kyle N. Weir, Ph.D., LMFT, is a Professor of Marriage, Family, and Child Counseling in the Counselor Education program at California State University—Fresno. He has also previously served as Chair of the Department of Counselor Education and Rehabilitation and as Coordinator of the Counselor Education program. He will begin his term as Director of Fresno Family Counseling Center – a student-training clinic operated by the faculty and students of Fresno State's Marriage, Family, and Child Counseling degree serving the needs of the California Central Valley community starting January 2022. He received a B.S. in Public Policy and Management, an M.A. in Sociology (Organizations), a M.M.F.T. in Marital & Family Therapy, and a Ph.D. in Sociology/Marriage and Family Therapy from the University of Southern California. He is a licensed marriage and family therapist in California, was a part-time clinician at LDS Family Services, and now practices with the firm Roubicek & Thacker, Inc. He also serves as the Clinical Director of LifeSTAR of the Central Valley through Roubicek and Thacker, Inc.

He is married to Allison Brown Weir, and they have six children: Kellie, Nathan, Samantha, Joshua, Jason, and Daniel. It was through the personal adoption experiences with his children that Dr. Weir developed an academic interest in play therapy with adoptive and foster families. His clinical and ecclesiastical experiences generated his interest in OCD/Scrupulosity. Dr. Weir is the author of numerous peer-reviewed journal articles and the books *Coming Out of the Adoptive Closet* (2003; University Press of America), *The Choice of a Lifetime:*

What You Need to Know Before Adopting (2011; NTI Upstream), *Intimacy, Identity, and Ice Cream: Teaching Teens and Young Adults to Live the Law of Chastity* (2016; Cedar Fort Publishing); *Why Repentance Matters* (2018, Finegold Creek Press); *Collaborating for Connection as a Couple (CAST Workbook 1)* (2021); *The TRAIL to Love (CAST Workbook 2)* (2021); and *Twelve Collaborative Tasks for Couples (CAST Workbook 3)* (2021). He has served in numerous Church callings, including as a missionary in the Australia Brisbane Mission, bishop of the Yosemite Ward, and a high councilor (once in the Arcadia, CA Stake and twice in the Fresno, CA West Stake). He currently serves as a seminary teacher, elder's quorum instructor, and teaches the temple preparation course in his ward.

For more information visit:
   www.drkyleweir.com

For clinical appointments or questions contact:
   Kyle N. Weir, PhD, LMFT
   Roubicek and Thacker, Inc. (Private Practice)
   1879 E. Fir Ave., Suite 103, Fresno, CA 93720
   559-323-8484
   https://roubicekandthacker.com/individual-couples-family-counseling

NOTES

PREFACE - S.O.S.: AN INTEGRATIVE MODEL FOR TREATING SCRUPULOSITY

1. Clark, D.A. (2020). *Cognitive-Behavioral Therapy for OCD and Its Subtypes*, 2nd Ed. New York, NY: Guilford Press, p. 13.
2. Abramowitz, J.S. (2006). The psychological treatment of obsessive-compulsive disorder, *The Canadian Journal of Psychiatry*, 51(7), pp. 407-416.
3. Clark, D.A. (2020). *Cognitive-Behavioral Therapy for OCD and Its Subtypes*, 2nd Ed. New York, NY: Guilford Press, p. 78.
4. Wilhelm, S., Berman, N. C., Keshaviah, A., Schwartz, R. A., & Steketee, G. (2015). Mechanisms of change in cognitive therapy for obsessive compulsive disorder: Role of maladaptive beliefs and schemas. *Behaviour Research and Therapy*, 65, 5–10. https://doi-org.hmlproxy.lib.csufresno.edu/10.1016/j.brat.2014.12.006
5. Clark, D.A. (2020). *Cognitive-Behavioral Therapy for OCD and Its Subtypes*, 2nd Ed. New York, NY: Guilford Press, p. 316.
6. Clark, D.A. (2020). *Cognitive-Behavioral Therapy for OCD and Its Subtypes*, 2nd Ed. New York, NY: Guilford Press, p. 316.
7. Schwartz, J.M. (1996). *Brain Lock: Free Yourself from Obsessive-Compulsive Behavior*. New York, NY: Harper Perennial.

INTRODUCTION – THE MANY FACES OF SCRUPULOSITY

1. * All names and other identifying information about individuals used as examples in this book have been changed to protect their confidentiality.
2. * All names and other identifying information about individuals used as examples in this book have been changed to protect their confidentiality.

1. TO WHOM SHALL WE GO? THOU HAST THE WORDS OF ETERNAL LIFE

1. Neil L. Andersen, "Whom the Lord Calls, the Lord Qualifies," *Ensign* April 1993, https://www.lds.org/general-conference/1993/04/whom-the-lord-calls-the-lord-qualifies?lang=eng.
2. Most state laws will require that the client or patient sign a release of information (ROI) so that the therapist and bishop can engage in co-consultation with one another. In addition to being codified in law, it is also simply good practice to

NOTES

ensure that the patient is aware of and agrees to the exceptions to confidentiality that co-consultation would require between the clinician and ecclesiastical leader. I strongly advise both the Church leader and the therapist obtain written releases of information from the patient/ward member before communicating confidential information with one another.

3. Weir, K.N., Greaves, M., Denno, R., Kelm, C., Ragu, R. (2014). Scrupulosity: Practical Treatment Considerations Drawn from Clinical and Ecclesiastical Experiences with Latter-day Saint Persons Struggling with Religiously-oriented Obsessive Compulsive Disorder, *Issues in Religion and Psychotherapy*, Vol. 36, No. 1, pp. 57-69.

   (Full references in text were omitted for readability, but the full quote can be found in the text of the article)

4. Abramowitz, J.S. & Jacoby, R.J. (2014). Scrupulosity: A cognitive-behavioral analysis and implications for treatment. *Journal of Obsessive-Compulsive and Related Disorders*. 3, 140-149.

5. American Psychiatric Association. (2013). Diagnostic and statistical manual of mental disorders (5th ed.). Washington, DC: APA, p. 237.

6. American Psychiatric Association. (2013). Diagnostic and statistical manual of mental disorders (5th ed.). Washington, DC: APA, p. 239.

7. National Institute of Mental Health (Nov. 2017), Obsessive-Compulsive Disorder (OCD). https://www.nimh.nih.gov/health/statistics/obsessive-compulsive-disorder-ocd.shtml

   See also:

   Morrison, Alexander B. (2003). *Valley of Sorrow: A Layman's Guide to Understanding Mental Illness*. Salt Lake City, UT: Deseret Book Company.

   Schwartz, J.M. (1996). *Brain Lock: Free Yourself from Obsessive-Compulsive Behavior*. New York, NY: Harper Perennial.

8. Abramowitz, J.S. & Jacoby, R.J. (2014). Scrupulosity: A cognitive-behavioral analysis and implications for treatment. *Journal of Obsessive-Compulsive and Related Disorders*. 3, 140-149.

9. Abramowitz, J.S. (2006). The psychological treatment of obsessive-compulsive disorder, *The Canadian Journal of Psychiatry*, 51(7), 407-416.

10. Twohig, M. P., Hayes, S. C., Plumb, J. C., Pruitt, L. D., Collins, A. B., Hazlett-Stevens, H., & Woidneck, M. R. (2010). A randomized clinical trial of acceptance and commitment therapy versus progressive relaxation training for obsessive-compulsive disorder. *Journal of consulting and clinical psychology*, 78(5), 705–716. doi:10.1037/a0020508

2. FAITH AS A PRINCIPLE OF ACTION AND POWER IN THE FACE OF UNCERTAINTY

1. Clark, D.A. (2020). *Cognitive-Behavioral Therapy for OCD and Its Subtypes*, 2nd Ed. New York, NY: Guilford Press, p. 27.

2. Clark, D.A. (2020). *Cognitive-Behavioral Therapy for OCD and Its Subtypes*, 2nd Ed. New York, NY: Guilford Press, p. 316.

   Abramowitz, J.S. & Jacoby, R.J. (2014). Scrupulosity: A cognitive-behavioral

analysis and implications for treatment. *Journal of Obsessive-Compulsive and Related Disorders*. 3, 140-149.
3. Ciarrocchi, J. W. (1995). *The Doubting Disease: Help for Scrupulosity and Religious Compulsions.* Mahwah, NJ: Paulist Press.
4. Russell M. Nelson, "Revelation for the Church, Revelation for Our Lives," April 2018 General Conference, https://www.lds.org/general-conference/2018/04/revelation-for-the-Church-revelation-for-our-lives?lang=eng.
5. Neil L. Anderson, "You Know Enough," Oct. 2008 General Conference, https://www.lds.org/general-conference/2008/10/you-know-enough?lang=eng.
6. Ciarrocchi, J. W. (1995). *The Doubting Disease: Help for Scrupulosity and Religious Compulsions.* Mahwah, NJ: Paulist Press.
7. Allen, G. E. K., & Wang, K. T. (2014). Examining religious commitment, perfectionism, scrupulosity, and well-being among LDS individuals. *Psychology of Religion and Spirituality*, 6(3), 257-264.
8. * Just as Abraham taught Isaac in Gen. 22: 8: "...God will provide himself a lamb for a burnt offering," the Savior provided *Himself* as an offering to not only redeem from sin but to heal infirmities like scrupulosity (see Alma 7: 11-14). The scrupulous must place their compulsions on the altar of sacrifice.
9. Dieter F. Uchtdorf, "Come, Join with Us," Oct. 2013 General Conference, https://www.lds.org/general-conference/2013/10/come-join-with-us?lang=eng.
10. Neil L. Anderson, "You Know Enough," Oct. 2008 General Conference, https://www.lds.org/general-conference/2008/10/you-know-enough?lang=eng.

3. PHASE I: FOUNDATIONAL TRUTHS AND THE GOSPEL OF GROWTH

1. Aaron West, "I Will Be Found of You," *Ensign*, January 2010, https://www.lds.org/ensign/2010/01/i-will-be-found-of-you?lang=eng.
2. Jeffrey R. Holland, "Come Unto Me," *Ensign*, April 1998, https://www.lds.org/ensign/1998/04/come-unto-me?lang=eng.
3. Dieter F. Uchtdorf, "Four Titles," April 2013 General Conference, https://www.lds.org/general-conference/2013/04/four-titles?lang=eng.
4. I also highly recommend the October 2018 General Conference talk, "The Father," by Elder Brian K. Ashton, who tenderly describes his wife's struggles with feeling "unworthy" despite her faithfulness and how developing a correct understanding of the nature and character of God helped her overcome these feelings.
5. Fiona Givens and Terryl Givens (2017). *The Christ Who Heals: How God Restored the Truth that Saves Us.* Salt Lake City, UT: Deseret Books.
6. Roger E. Olson (1999). *The Story of Christian Theology*, as cited in Fiona Givens and Terryl Givens, (2017). *The Christ Who Heals: How God Restored the Truth that Saves Us.* Salt Lake City, UT: Deseret Books, p. 23.
7. Fiona Givens and Terryl Givens (2017). *The Christ Who Heals: How God Restored the Truth that Saves Us.* Salt Lake City, UT: Deseret Books, p. 23.
8. Fiona Givens and Terryl Givens (2017). *The Christ Who Heals: How God Restored the Truth that Saves Us.* Salt Lake City, UT: Deseret Books, p. 23.
9. S. Michael Wilcox (2020). What Seek Ye? Salt Lake City, UT: Deseret Books.

NOTES

10. Cefalu, P. (2010). The doubting disease: Religious scrupulosity and obsessive-compulsive disorder in historical context. Journal of Medical Humanities, 31(2), 111–125.
11. Cefalu, P. (2010). The doubting disease: Religious scrupulosity and obsessive-compulsive disorder in historical context. Journal of Medical Humanities, 31(2), 111–125.
12. Bouwsma, W.J. (1984). John Calvin's Anxiety. *Proceedings of the American Philosophical Society* Vol. 128, No. 3 (Sep., 1984), pp. 252-256, Published by: American Philosophical Society, https://www.jstor.org/stable/986886
13. Jonathan Edwards (1741). Sinners in the Hands of an Angry God. As cited in Baym, N. & Levine, R.S. (Eds.) (2013). *The Norton Anthology of American Literature*, Shorter 8th Ed. New York, NY: W.W. Norton & Co., pp. 209-220.
14. Jonathan Edwards (1741). Sinners in the Hands of an Angry God. As cited in Baym, N. & Levine, R.S. (Eds.) (2013). *The Norton Anthology of American Literature*, Shorter 8th Ed. New York, NY: W.W. Norton & Co., pp. 209-220.
15. Jonathan Edwards (1741). Sinners in the Hands of an Angry God. As cited in Baym, N. & Levine, R.S. (Eds.) (2013). *The Norton Anthology of American Literature*, Shorter 8th Ed. New York, NY: W.W. Norton & Co., pp. 209-220.
16. Fiona Givens and Terryl Givens (2017). *The Christ Who Heals: How God Restored the Truth that Saves Us.* Salt Lake City, UT: Deseret Books, p. 40.
17. Fiona Givens and Terryl Givens (2017). *The Christ Who Heals: How God Restored the Truth that Saves Us.* Salt Lake City, UT: Deseret Books, p. 42.
18. Lewis, C.S. (1942/2001). *The Screwtape Letters*, New York, NY: HarperCollins, pp. 37-41.
19. Bruce C. Hafen, "The Atonement: All for All," April 2004 General Conference, https://www.lds.org/general-conference/2004/04/the-atonement-all-for-all?lang=eng
20. Dallin H. Oaks, "Good, Better, Best," October 2007 General Conference, https://www.lds.org/general-conference/2007/10/good-better-best?lang=eng
21. Theodore Roosevelt, "Citizenship in a Republic," 23 Feb. 1910, http://www.theodore-roosevelt.com/images/research/speeches/maninthearena.pdf
22. Jeffrey R. Holland, "Be Ye Therefore Perfect – Eventually," October 2017 General Conference., https://www.lds.org/general-conference/2017/10/be-ye-therefore-perfect-eventually?lang=eng&country=nz.

4. THE QUESTIONS THAT HAUNT THE SCRUPULOUS: PERFECTIONISM, SUFFICIENCY IN REPENTANCE THROUGH COVENANT RELATIONSHIPS, AND JUDGING

1. See Moses 4:1 and Doctrine and Covenants 29:36.
2. Andrew Skinner (2016). *To Become Like God: Witnesses of Our Divine Potential.* Salt Lake City, UT: Deseret Books.
3. Clark, D.A. (2020). *Cognitive-Behavioral Therapy for OCD and Its Subtypes*, 2nd Ed. New York, NY: Guilford Press, p. 27.

4. Allen, G. E. K., Wang, K. T., & Stokes, H. (2015). Examining legalism, scrupulosity, family perfectionism, and psychological adjustment among LDS individuals. *Mental Health, Religion & Culture*, 18(4), 246–258.
5. Stoeber, J., & Otto, K. (2006). Positive conceptions of perfectionism: Approaches, evidence, challenges. *Personality and Social Psychology Review*, 10(4), 295–319.
    Wu, T. & Wei, M. (2008). Perfectionism and negative mood: The mediating roles of validation from others versus self. *Journal of Counseling Psychology*, 55(2), 276-288.
6. Wu, T. & Wei, M. (2008). Perfectionism and negative mood: The mediating roles of validation from others versus self. *Journal of Counseling Psychology*, 55(2), 276-288.
7. Allen, G. E. K., Wang, K. T., & Stokes, H. (2015). Examining legalism, scrupulosity, family perfectionism, and psychological adjustment among LDS individuals. *Mental Health, Religion & Culture*, 18(4), 246–258.
    Allen, G. E. K., & Wang, K. T. (2014). Examining religious commitment, perfectionism, scrupulosity, and well-being among LDS individuals. *Psychology of Religion and Spirituality*, 6(3), 257–264.
8. Stoeber, J., Madigan, D.J., & Gonidis, L. (2020). Perfectionism is adaptive, but what's the combined effect? *Personality and Individual Differences*, 161, 109846.
9. Allen, G. E. K., Wang, K. T., & Stokes, H. (2015). Examining legalism, scrupulosity, family perfectionism, and psychological adjustment among LDS individuals. *Mental Health, Religion & Culture*, 18(4), 246–258.
    Allen, G. E. K., & Wang, K. T. (2014). Examining religious commitment, perfectionism, scrupulosity, and well-being among LDS individuals. *Psychology of Religion and Spirituality*, 6(3), 257–264.
10. Dweck, C.S. (2006). *Mindset: The New Psychology of Success*. New York, NY: Ballantine Books.
11. Allen, G. E. K., Wang, K. T., & Stokes, H. (2015). Examining legalism, scrupulosity, family perfectionism, and psychological adjustment among LDS individuals. *Mental Health, Religion & Culture*, 18(4), 246–258.
    Allen, G. E. K., & Wang, K. T. (2014). Examining religious commitment, perfectionism, scrupulosity, and well-being among LDS individuals. *Psychology of Religion and Spirituality*, 6(3), 257–264.
12. The material (pp. 57-62 of this book) surrounding the discussion of the parable by Stephen Robinson and the Parable of the Socks is excerpted from the book *Why Repentance Matters* (Weir, 2018, Finegold Creek Press) and is used with permission.
13. Stephen Robinson, (1992). *Believing Christ: The Parable of the Bicycle and Other Good News*. Salt Lake City, UT: Deseret Book.
14. Bruce R. McConkie, "The Purifying Power of Gethsemane," General Conference, April 1985, https://www.lds.org/general-conference/1985/04/the-purifying-power-of-gethsemane?lang=eng.
15. Neal A. Maxwell, "Enduring Well," *Ensign* April 1997, https://www.lds.org/ensign/1997/04/enduring-well?lang=eng.
16. Wilcox, B. (2013). *The Continuous Conversion: God Isn't Just Proving Us, He's Improving Us*. Salt Lake City, UT: Deseret Book, p. 24.
17. See Ephesians 5:23-26; Hosea 1:2, and Matt. 25:1-13 as just a few examples.
18. Tad Walch, (May 4, 2018). "Covenant Belonging" is a Key Part of Ministering, Elder Gong Says at BYU Women's Conference, Deseret News, https://www.

NOTES

deseretnews.com/article/900017812/covenant-belonging-a-key-part-of-ministering-elder-gong-says-at-byu-womens-conference.html

19. Tad Walch, (May 4, 2018). "Covenant Belonging" is a Key Part of Ministering, Elder Gong Says at BYU Women's Conference, Deseret News, https://www.deseretnews.com/article/900017812/covenant-belonging-a-key-part-of-ministering-elder-gong-says-at-byu-womens-conference.html
20. See Jeremiah 1, Isaiah 6, Moses 6: 26-34, 1 Samuel 3, Moses 1:1-6
21. Russell M. Nelson, "Perfection Pending," General Conference Oct. 1995, https://www.lds.org/general-conference/1995/10/perfection-pending?lang=eng
22. Compare Matthew 5:48 to 3 Nephi 12:48 and you will see the Savior included Himself with His Father as perfect only after He was resurrected.
23. Jeffrey R. Holland, "Be Ye Therefore Perfect – Eventually," October 2017 General Conference., https://www.lds.org/general-conference/2017/10/be-ye-therefore-perfect-eventually?lang=eng&country=nz.
24. Wilcox, B. (2009). *The Continuous Atonement: Christ Doesn't Just Make Up the Difference, He Makes All the Difference.* Salt Lake City, UT: Deseret Book, pp. 47-49.
25. "Meet Our New Prophet!" *Friend* Magazine, March 2018, https://www.lds.org/friend/2018/03/meet-our-new-prophet?lang=eng
26. Gerrit W. Gong, "Our Campfire of Faith," Oct. 2018 General Conference, https://www.lds.org/general-conference/2018/10/our-campfire-of-faith?lang=eng.
27. Gerrit W. Gong, "Our Campfire of Faith," Oct. 2018 General Conference.
28. Gerrit W. Gong, "Our Campfire of Faith," Oct. 2018 General Conference.
29. Nothing in this chapter or book should be misconstrued as suggesting full and complete repentance is not a necessary part of redemption, salvation, and exaltation. But with the scrupulous Latter-day Saints, it has been my experience that they are sincerely repentant and comply with God's conditions of repentance. It is their OCD that prevents them from having the peace of conscience and peace of mind that comes through repentance. They worry excessively about miniscule issues that are really not about repentance, per se, but about aspects of imperfection in themselves made larger than realistically expected of anyone truly repenting.
30. David A. Bednar, "Gather Together in One All Things in Christ," Oct. 2018 General Conference, https://www.lds.org/general-conference/2018/10/gather-together-in-one-all-things-in-christ?lang=eng.
31. Russell M. Nelson, "We Can Do Better," April 2019 General Conference, https://www.lds.org/general-conference/2019/04/36nelson?lang=eng.
32. See https://judaism.stackexchange.com/questions/35359/what-is-the-role-of-a-shofet-as-in-the-book-of-shoftim, Retrieved July 4, 2018.
33. See https://www.britannica.com/topic/biblical-literature/The-Nevi-im-Prophets#ref597691, Retrieved July 4, 2018.
34. See http://biblehub.com/lexicon/judges/2-16.htm, Retrieved July 4, 2018.
35. See Hirsch, E.G. and Ryssel, V. (2011). "Judges, Book of," Jewish Encyclopedia, http://www.jewishencyclopedia.com/articles/9051-judges-book-of, Retrieved July 4, 2018.
36. See http://www.abarim-publications.com/Meaning/Daniel.html#.Wz51YI6ovxs;
    The following description is given about the ancient use of the verb "din" in an informal manner compared to the modern use of "beit din" or rabbinical court that conveys more formality:

"Still, there doesn't seem to be a special meaning to our verb דין (*din*). It's used in the more poetic passages, and it was probably an old fashioned word by the time the Bible was written in its final form. That we know because the number of names derived from this verb seems disproportional to the frequency it occurs in the Hebrew narrative text. Names, after all, are often passed on from person to person without following changes in language and are therefore usually older than current language forms.

"This indicates that our verb describes a more natural government by people who are naturally equipped to lead (folks who are wise and strong), in contrast to the governing done by some formal government, which consists of folks that obtained their positions through their abilities to please the king."

37. See http://www.jewishencyclopedia.com/articles/9051-judges-book-of, Retrieved July 4, 2018.
38. Regarding how judges were supposed to deliver justice to the oppressed and rescue or deliver the Lord's people from defeat or destruction see http://biblehub.com/hebrew/1840.htm, Retrieved July 4, 2018.
39. The more commonly used Hebrew name for "God is my Salvation" is Elisha – see http://biblehub.com/hebrew/477.htm; Daniel more literally translates as "God is my Judge" but in Hebrew the concepts of judge, savior, deliverer, and rescuer are inseparable.
40. See https://www.hsutx.edu/hsubb/learningobjects/overviewoftheoldtestament/pages/51.html;

    From Hardin-Simmons University Website – "Judge: The word translated 'judge' literally means 'savior' or 'deliverer' in Hebrew. The OT judges are quite distinct from modern judges. They were primarily military heroes who led a particular tribe into battle against an oppressor. The judges did not perform judicial duties, with the exception of Deborah who settled disputes under her palm tree (Judg. 4:5). However, after delivering Israel militarily, a judge did function as the primary leader of his/her region and may have performed judicial functions in that capacity (though the text of Judges never specifies this)."
41. J. Reuben Clark, Jr., General Conference Oct. 1953, as cited in "Mercy – The Divine Gift, Thomas S. Monson, April 1995 General Conference, https://www.lds.org/general-conference/1995/04/mercy-the-divine-gift?lang=eng.

5. "GOD-ATTACHMENT" AND FAMILY OF ORIGIN WORK

1. * All names and other identifying information about individuals used as examples in this book have been changed to protect their confidentiality.
2. Vitz, P. (1999, 2013 2nd Ed.). *Faith of the fatherless: The psychology of atheism*. San Francisco, CA: Ignatius Press.
3. Vitz, P. (1999, 2013 2nd Ed.). *Faith of the fatherless: The psychology of atheism*. San Francisco, CA: Ignatius Press.
4. The phrase "God is dead" first appeared in Nietzche's writings in his collection *The Gay Science* (1882) as was translated into English thusly:

    "God is dead. God remains dead. And we have killed him. How shall we comfort

NOTES

ourselves, the murderers of all murderers? What was holiest and mightiest of all that the world has yet owned has bled to death under our knives: who will wipe this blood off us? What water is there for us to clean ourselves? What festivals of atonement, what sacred games shall we have to invent? Is not the greatness of this deed too great for us? Must we ourselves not become gods simply to appear worthy of it?" — Nietzsche, *The Gay Science, Section 125, tr. Walter Kaufmann* (See Kaufmann, W. (1974). *Nietzche: Philosopher, Psychologist, Antichrist.* Princeton, NJ: Princeton University Press).

But the phrase "God is dead" was made famous by Nietzsche's book *Thus Spoke Zarathustra* (See Nietzsche, Friedrich Wilhelm (Translated by Adrian Del Caro, edited by Robert Pippin.) (2006). *Thus spoke Zarathustra: A book for all and none.* Cambridge, MA: Cambridge University Press).

5. See Vitz, P. (1999). *Faith of the fatherless: The psychology of atheism.* San Francisco, CA: Ignatius Press, pp. 47-48, as well as "7 Disturbing Facts about Sigmund Freud" at https://medium.com/@suriana/7-disturbing-facts-about-sigmund-freud-4a8c586c780f.
6. Allen, G. E. K., Wang, K. T., & Stokes, H. (2015). Examining legalism, scrupulosity, family perfectionism, and psychological adjustment among LDS individuals. *Mental Health, Religion & Culture,* 18(4), 246–258.
7. Givens, T. & Givens, F. (2012) *The God who weeps: How Mormonism makes sense of life.* Salt Lake City, UT: Ensign Peak, p. 58.
8. Clinton, T. and Straub, J (2010). *God attachment: Why you believe, act, and feel the way you do about God.* New York, NY: Howard Books.
9. Clinton, T. and Straub, J (2010). *God attachment: Why you believe, act, and feel the way you do about God.* New York, NY: Howard Books, p. 69.
10. Clinton, T. and Straub, J (2010). *God attachment: Why you believe, act, and feel the way you do about God.* New York, NY: Howard Books, p. 72.
11. * All names and other identifying information about individuals used as examples in this book have been changed to protect their confidentiality.
12. * All names and other identifying information about individuals used as examples in this book have been changed to protect their confidentiality.
13. Russell M. Nelson, "Revelation for the Church, Revelation for our Lives," April 2018 General Conference.
14. See Brent L. Top and Bruce A. Chadwick, "Helping Teens Stay Strong," *Ensign,* March 1999, p. 27, for an interesting study that showed that teens' personal prayer, scripture study, and fasting were more influential on righteous living than family prayer, scripture study, and even Church attendance.
15. Smith Jr., Joseph "The King Follett Sermon" as cited in *Ensign* (April and May 1971).
16. Fowler, J. (1981). *Stages of Faith: The Psychology of Human Development and the Quest for Meaning.* San Francisco, CA: Harper & Row.
17. Clark, D.A. (2020). *Cognitive-Behavioral Therapy for OCD and Its Subtypes,* 2nd Ed. New York, NY: Guilford Press, p. 316.
18. Browne, H. A., Gair, S. L., Scharf, J. M., & Grice, D. E. (2014). Genetics of obsessive-compulsive disorder and related disorders. *Psychiatric Clinics of North America,* 37(3), 319–335. https://doi-org.hmlproxy.lib.csufresno.edu/10.1016/j.psc.2014.06.002

NOTES

19. See the following sources on the debate concerning the existence and causes of OCD subtyping:
    Radomsky, A. S., & Taylor, S. (2005). Subtyping OCD: Prospects and Problems. *Behavior Therapy, 36*(4), 371–379. https://doi-org.hmlproxy.lib.csufresno.edu/10.1016/S0005-7894(05)80119-4
    Rowsell, M., & Francis, S. E. (2015). OCD subtypes: Which, if any, are valid? *Clinical Psychology: Science and Practice, 22*(4), 414–435. https://doi-org.hmlproxy.lib.csufresno.edu/10.1111/cpsp.12130
    von Strunck, H. (2016). Exploration of the relationship between OCD and parenting style subtypes [ProQuest Information & Learning]. In *Dissertation Abstracts International: Section B: The Sciences and Engineering* (Vol. 77, Issue 6–B(E)).
    Vorstenbosch, V., Hood, H. K., Rogojanski, J., Antony, M. M., Summerfeldt, L. J., & McCabe, R. E. (2012). Exploring the relationship between ocd symptom subtypes and domains of functional impairment. *Journal of Obsessive-Compulsive and Related Disorders, 1*(1), 33–40. https://doi-org.hmlproxy.lib.csufresno.edu/10.1016/j.jocrd.2011.10.002
20. Fowler, J. (1981). *Stages of Faith: The Psychology of Human Development and the Quest for Meaning.* San Francisco, CA: Harper & Row, p. 121.
21. Fowler, J. (1981). *Stages of Faith: The Psychology of Human Development and the Quest for Meaning.* San Francisco, CA: Harper & Row, p. 132.
22. Fowler, J. (1981). *Stages of Faith: The Psychology of Human Development and the Quest for Meaning.* San Francisco, CA: Harper & Row, p. 132.
23. Fowler, J. (1981). *Stages of Faith: The Psychology of Human Development and the Quest for Meaning.* San Francisco, CA: Harper & Row, p. 133.
24. Neil L. Andersen, "Tell Me the Stories of Jesus," April 2010 General Conference, https://www.lds.org/general-conference/2010/04/tell-me-the-stories-of-jesus?lang=eng.
25. Fowler, J. (1981). *Stages of Faith: The Psychology of Human Development and the Quest for Meaning.* San Francisco, CA: Harper & Row, p. 139.
26. See Joseph Smith-History, Doctrine and Covenants 130:22, Doctrine and Covenants 76, and Genesis 1:26-27.
27. Fowler, J. (1981). *Stages of Faith: The Psychology of Human Development and the Quest for Meaning.* San Francisco, CA: Harper & Row, p. 143.
28. See Alma 42:13-16 and 23-26.
29. See Enos 1:6 and Ether 3:12.
30. J. Reuben Clark, Jr., General Conference Oct. 1953, as cited in "Mercy – The Divine Gift, Thomas S. Monson, April 1995 General Conference, https://www.lds.org/general-conference/1995/04/mercy-the-divine-gift?lang=eng.
31. See Helaman 5:11
32. Fowler, J. (1981). *Stages of Faith: The Psychology of Human Development and the Quest for Meaning.* San Francisco, CA: Harper & Row, p. 150.
33. Allen, G. E. K., Wang, K. T., & Stokes, H. (2015). Examining legalism, scrupulosity, family perfectionism, and psychological adjustment among LDS individuals. *Mental Health, Religion & Culture, 18*(4), 246–258.
34. See Michelle D. Craig, "Divine Discontent," Oct. 2018 General conference; and Russell M. Nelson, in Tad Walch, "'The Lord's Message Is for Everyone': President Nelson Talks about Global Tour," *Deseret News,* Apr. 12, 2018, deseretnews.com.

NOTES

35. Richard G. Scott, "Peace of Conscience and Peace of Mind," Oct. 2004 General Conference), https://www.lds.org/general-conference/2004/10/peace-of-conscience-and-peace-of-mind?lang=eng
36. Fowler, J. (1981). *Stages of Faith: The Psychology of Human Development and the Quest for Meaning.* San Francisco, CA: Harper & Row, p. 153.
37. Fowler, J. (1981). *Stages of Faith: The Psychology of Human Development and the Quest for Meaning.* San Francisco, CA: Harper & Row, p. 173.
38. Allen, G. E. K., Wang, K. T., & Stokes, H. (2015). Examining legalism, scrupulosity, family perfectionism, and psychological adjustment among LDS individuals. *Mental Health, Religion & Culture,* 18(4), 246–258.

    See also: Wu, T. & Wei, M. (2008). Perfectionism and negative mood: The mediating roles of validation from others versus self. *Journal of Counseling Psychology,* 55(2), 276-288.
39. Fowler, J. (1981). *Stages of Faith: The Psychology of Human Development and the Quest for Meaning.* San Francisco, CA: Harper & Row, p. 179.
40. Fowler, J. (1981). *Stages of Faith: The Psychology of Human Development and the Quest for Meaning.* San Francisco, CA: Harper & Row, p. 182.
41. Clark, D.A. (2020). *Cognitive-Behavioral Therapy for OCD and Its Subtypes,* 2nd Ed. New York, NY: Guilford Press, p. 317.
42. Fowler, J. (1981). *Stages of Faith: The Psychology of Human Development and the Quest for Meaning.* San Francisco, CA: Harper & Row, p. 185.
43. Fowler, J. (1981). *Stages of Faith: The Psychology of Human Development and the Quest for Meaning.* San Francisco, CA: Harper & Row, p. 184.
44. Fowler, J. (1981). *Stages of Faith: The Psychology of Human Development and the Quest for Meaning.* San Francisco, CA: Harper & Row, p. 200.
45. Fowler, J. (1981). *Stages of Faith: The Psychology of Human Development and the Quest for Meaning.* San Francisco, CA: Harper & Row, p. 200.
46. Jesus, in the New Testament, was quite a "rule breaker" of the hypocritical societal rules of His day from the perspective of the Pharisees and Saducees. He broke the social conventions of the Pharisees and Saducees. Why? Jesus broke the Pharisees' and Sadducee's rules because they were misapplications of the true doctrines and principles that He taught and commanded them to follow. It was Jesus (as the premortal Jehovah) that commanded Moses and the children of Israel, "Remember the sabbath day, to keep it holy" (Exodus 20:8). When the Pharisees attacked Jesus, the Great Lawgiver, for healing on the sabbath or letting his disciples eat corn from the field on the holy day, His retort wasn't to suggest keeping the sabbath day holy wasn't an important commandment – rather it was to instruct them that they had misapplied the doctrines and principles regarding the sabbath in their rules about the sabbath. We must focus more on doctrines and principles, rather than being caught up in the myopia of rules – for they are often misapplications in our day – and strive to apply the doctrines and principles righteously. The scrupulous often focus more on the rules (and misapply the doctrines and principles). Shifting their focus to higher and holier ways (doctrines and principles) often helps ameliorate scrupulosity symptoms.
47. Bruce C. Hafen, "The Atonement: All for All," April 2004 General Conference, https://www.lds.org/general-conference/2004/04/the-atonement-all-for-all?lang=eng.

48. Bruce C. Hafen, "The Atonement: All for All," April 2004 General Conference, https://www.lds.org/general-conference/2004/04/the-atonement-all-for-all?lang=eng
49. Russell M. Nelson, "Perfection Pending," General Conference Oct. 1995, https://www.lds.org/general-conference/1995/10/perfection-pending?lang=eng

6. MINDFUL SELF-COMPASSION AND THE COMPASSION OF CHRIST

1. Neff, Kristen (2011). *Self-Compassion: The Proven Power of Being Kind to Yourself*, New York, NY: William Morrow, an imprint of HarperCollins.
    McGonigal, Kelly (2016). *The Science of Compassion: A Modern Approach for Cultivating Empathy, Love, and Connection*. (Audiobook). Louisville, CO: Sounds True Publishing.
    Harris, Russ. (2019). *ACT Made Simple: An Easy-to-Read Primer on Acceptance and Commitment Therapy*. Oakland, CA: New Harbinger Publications, Inc.
2. There is a HUGE difference between guilt and shame. Guilt is a healthy acknowledgement of one's mistakes, poor choices, or bad behavior. Shame is about feeling worthless and devalued as a person. Guilt focuses on behavior (and therefore also about changing behavior), but shame focuses on identity and personhood. The difference can be seen in the statements: "I made a mistake" (Guilt) vs. "I am a mistake" (Shame). Shameful self-talk (for example, "I'm such a loser for XYZ reasons" or "I'm an idiot" or even "I'm worthless") is meant to lead to change, but research shows that paradoxically is has the opposite effect. Guilt leads to godly sorrow or the sorrow unto change, but shame is usually the engine that drives cyclical habitual failings and addictions.
3. Stoeber, J., Lalova, A. V., & Lumley, E. J. (2019). Perfectionism, (self-)compassion, and subjective well-being: A mediation model. *Personality and Individual Differences*. https://doi-org.hmlproxy.lib.csufresno.edu/10.1016/j.paid.2019.109708
4. Merritt, O. A., & Purdon, C. L. (2020). Scared of compassion: Fear of compassion in anxiety, mood, and non-clinical groups. *British Journal of Clinical Psychology*, 59(3), 354–368. https://doi-org.hmlproxy.lib.csufresno.edu/10.1111/bjc.12250
5. Chase, T. E., Chasson, G. S., Hamilton, C. E., Wetterneck, C. T., Smith, A. H., & Hart, J. M. (2019). The mediating role of emotion regulation difficulties in the relationship between self-compassion and OCD severity in a non-referred sample. *Journal of Cognitive Psychotherapy*, 33(2), 157–168. https://doi-org.hmlproxy.lib.csufresno.edu/10.1891/0889-8391.33.2.157
    Eichholz, A., Schwartz, C., Meule, A., Heese, J., Neumüller, J., & Voderholzer, U. (2020). Self-compassion and emotion regulation difficulties in obsessive–compulsive disorder. *Clinical Psychology & Psychotherapy*. https://doi-org.hmlproxy.lib.csufresno.edu/10.1002/cpp.2451
    Wetterneck, C. T., Lee, E. B., Smith, A. H., & Hart, J. M. (2013). Courage, self-compassion, and values in obsessive-compulsive disorder. *Journal of Contextual Behavioral Science*, 2(3–4), 68–73. https://doi-org.hmlproxy.lib.csufresno.edu/10.1016/j.jcbs.2013.09.002
6. Neff, Kristen (2011). *Self-Compassion: The Proven Power of Being Kind to Yourself*, New York, NY: William Morrow, an imprint of HarperCollins.

NOTES

> McGonigal, Kelly (2016). *The Science of Compassion: A Modern Approach for Cultivating Empathy, Love, and Connection.* (Audiobook). Louisville, CO: Sounds True Publishing.
>
> Harris, Russ. (2019). *ACT Made Simple: An Easy-to-Read Primer on Acceptance and Commitment Therapy.* Oakland, CA: New Harbinger Publications, Inc.

7. Key, B. L., Rowa, K., Bieling, P., McCabe, R., & Pawluk, E. J. (2017). Mindfulness-based cognitive therapy as an augmentation treatment for obsessive–compulsive disorder. *Clinical Psychology & Psychotherapy, 24*(5), 1109–1120. https://doi-org.hmlproxy.lib.csufresno.edu/10.1002/cpp.2076

   > Leeuwerik, T., Cavanagh, K., & Strauss, C. (2020). The association of trait mindfulness and self-compassion with obsessive-compulsive disorder symptoms: Results from a large survey with treatment-seeking adults. *Cognitive Therapy and Research, 44*(1), 120–135. https://doi-org.hmlproxy.lib.csufresno.edu/10.1007/s10608-019-10049-4

8. Diaphragmatic breathing helps reduce anxiety by switching the person utilizing this tool from the sympathetic nervous system to the parasympathetic nervous system. It requires deep breaths using the stomach muscles and the diaphragm as opposed to shallow chest only breathing which actually stimulates more anxiety. I often tell patients to "imagine if someone was about to punch you in the gut. What muscles would you tighten? Those are the muscles you should be using when practicing diaphragmatic breathing." This is a powerful tool in emotional regulation, as well.

9. Clark, D.A. (2020). *Cognitive-Behavioral Therapy for OCD and Its Subtypes,* 2nd Ed. New York, NY: Guilford Press, p. 317.

10. Hobbes, Thomas (1968). *Leviathan.* Baltimore, MD: Penguin Books, Part 1, Chapter 13.

11. Jeffrey R. Holland, "Come Unto Me," *Ensign,* April 1998, https://www.lds.org/ensign/1998/04/come-unto-me?lang=eng.

12. See Tad R. Callister (2000). *The Infinite Atonement.* Salt Lake City, UT: Deseret Book Company for one of the best works on the subject

7. PHASE II: COGNITIVE BEHAVIORAL THERAPY TREATMENTS FOR OCD AND SCRUPULOSITY

1. IOCDF. "Medications for OCD." https://iocdf.org/about-ocd/ocd-treatment/meds/, Retrieved 4-1-19.
2. * All names and other identifying information about individuals used as examples in this book have been changed to protect their confidentiality
3. * Note that I'm using the word "feel" in this instance in the sense of an emotional relief from his obsessive anxieties.
4. * All names and other identifying information about individuals used as examples in this book have been changed to protect their confidentiality.
5. Schwartz, J.M. (1996). *Brain Lock: Free Yourself from Obsessive-Compulsive Behavior.* New York, NY: Harper Perennial.

   > Schwartz, J.M. and Gladding, R. (2011). *You are Not Your Brain: The 4-Step Solu-*

NOTES

tion for Changing Bad Habits, Ending Unhealthy Thinking, and Taking Control of Your Life. New York, NY: Penguin Group.
6. Schwartz, J.M. (1996). *Brain Lock: Free Yourself from Obsessive-Compulsive Behavior.* New York, NY: Harper Perennial.
7. Schwartz, J.M. (1996). *Brain Lock: Free Yourself from Obsessive-Compulsive Behavior.* New York, NY: Harper Perennial.
   Schwartz, J.M. and Gladding, R. (2011). *You are Not Your Brain: The 4-Step Solution for Changing Bad Habits, Ending Unhealthy Thinking, and Taking Control of Your Life.* New York, NY: Penguin Group.
8. Schwartz, J.M. (1996). *Brain Lock: Free Yourself from Obsessive-Compulsive Behavior.* New York, NY: Harper Perennial.
9. Schwartz, J.M. (1996). *Brain Lock: Free Yourself from Obsessive-Compulsive Behavior.* New York, NY: Harper Perennial.
10. * In his earlier book, *Brain Lock*, Dr. Schwartz uses the term "Reattribute" but in his later book he changed the second step to "Reframe" which seems easier for some people to remember.
11. Schwartz, J.M. (1996). *Brain Lock: Free Yourself from Obsessive-Compulsive Behavior.* New York, NY: Harper Perennial.
12. Schwartz, J. M., & Begley, S. (2002). *The mind & the brain: Neuroplasticity and the power of mental force.* New York, NY: Regan Books/Harper Collins Publishers.
    On page 89 of this book, Dr. Schwartz shows PET scans of the brain showing decreased energy activity in the right caudate nucleus – one of the key portions of the brain that gets "locked" during OCD obsessions – after ten weeks of the patient using his four-step regimen.
13. Segal, Z., Teasdale, J., Williams, M. (2002). *Mindfulness-Based Cognitive Therapy for Depression.* New York: Guilford Press.
    Maric, M., Willard, C., Wrzesien, M., & Bögels, S. M. (2019). Innovations in the treatment of childhood anxiety disorders: Mindfulness and self-compassion approaches. In L. J. Farrell, T. H. Ollendick, & P. Muris (Eds.), *Innovations in CBT for childhood anxiety, OCD, and PTSD: Improving access and outcomes.* (pp. 265–286). Cambridge University Press. https://doi-org.hmlproxy.lib.csufresno.edu/10.1017/9781108235655.013
14. Key, B. L., Rowa, K., Bieling, P., McCabe, R., & Pawluk, E. J. (2017). Mindfulness-based cognitive therapy as an augmentation treatment for obsessive–compulsive disorder. *Clinical Psychology & Psychotherapy, 24*(5), 1109–1120. https://doi-org.hmlproxy.lib.csufresno.edu/10.1002/cpp.2076
    Leeuwerik, T., Cavanagh, K., & Strauss, C. (2020). The association of trait mindfulness and self-compassion with obsessive-compulsive disorder symptoms: Results from a large survey with treatment-seeking adults. *Cognitive Therapy and Research, 44*(1), 120–135. https://doi-org.hmlproxy.lib.csufresno.edu/10.1007/s10608-019-10049-4
15. Barnard, P.J. & Teasdale, J.D. (1991). Interacting cognitive subsystems: A systemic approach to cognitive-affective interaction and change. *Cognition and Emotion,* 5(1) 1-39.
16. Allen, G. E. K., Wang, K. T., & Stokes, H. (2015). Examining legalism, scrupulosity, family perfectionism, and psychological adjustment among LDS individuals. *Mental Health, Religion & Culture,* 18(4), 246–258.
    Allen, G. E. K., & Wang, K. T. (2014). Examining religious commitment, perfec-

NOTES

tionism, scrupulosity, and well-being among LDS individuals. *Psychology of Religion and Spirituality*, 6(3), 257–264.
17. Troy, A. S., Shallcross, A. J., Davis, T. S., & Mauss, I. B. (2013). History of mindfulness-based cognitive therapy is associated with increased cognitive reappraisal ability. *Mindfulness*, 4(3), 213–222. https://doi-org.hmlproxy.lib.csufresno.edu/10.1007/s12671-012-0114-5
18. Wilhelm, S., Berman, N. C., Keshaviah, A., Schwartz, R. A., & Steketee, G. (2015). Mechanisms of change in cognitive therapy for obsessive compulsive disorder: Role of maladaptive beliefs and schemas. *Behaviour Research and Therapy*, 65, 5–10. https://doi-org.hmlproxy.lib.csufresno.edu/10.1016/j.brat.2014.12.006
19. Van Dam, N. T., van Vugt, M. K., Vago, D. R., Schmalzl, L., Saron, C. D., Olendzki, A., Meissner, T., Lazar, S. W., Kerr, C. E., Gorchov, J., Fox, K. C. R., Field, B. A., Britton, W. B., Brefczynski-Lewis, J. A., & Meyer, D. E. (2018). Mind the hype: A critical evaluation and prescriptive agenda for research on mindfulness and meditation. *Perspectives on Psychological Science*, 13(1), 36–61. https://doi-org.hmlproxy.lib.csufresno.edu/10.1177/1745691617709589
20. Abramowitz, J.S. (2018). *Getting over OCD: A 10-step workbook for taking back your life*, 2nd ed. New York, NY: Guilford Press.
    Abramowitz, J.S., Deacon, B.J., and Whiteside, S.P.H. (2019). *Exposure Therapy for Anxiety: Principles and Practice*, 2nd ed. New York, NY: Guilford Press.

8. EXPOSURE AND RESPONSE PREVENTION AND SCRUPULOSITY

1. Abramowitz, J.S. (2006). The psychological treatment of obsessive-compulsive disorder, *The Canadian Journal of Psychiatry*, 51(7), pp. 407-416.
2. Clark, D.A. (2020). *Cognitive-Behavioral Therapy for OCD and Its Subtypes*, 2nd Ed. New York, NY: Guilford Press, p. 78.
3. Wilhelm, S., Berman, N. C., Keshaviah, A., Schwartz, R. A., & Steketee, G. (2015). Mechanisms of change in cognitive therapy for obsessive compulsive disorder: Role of maladaptive beliefs and schemas. *Behaviour Research and Therapy*, 65, 5–10. https://doi-org.hmlproxy.lib.csufresno.edu/10.1016/j.brat.2014.12.006
4.
5. Clark, D.A. (2020). *Cognitive-Behavioral Therapy for OCD and Its Subtypes*, 2nd Ed. New York, NY: Guilford Press, p. 336.
   Alonso, P., Menchon, J.M., Pifarre, J., Mataix-Cols, D., Torres, L. Salgado, P., et al. (2001) Long-term follow-up and predictors of clinical outcome in obsessive-compulsive patients treated with serotonin reuptake inhibitors and behavioral therapy. *Journal of Clinical Psychiatry*, 62, 535-540.
6. Clark, D.A. (2020). *Cognitive-Behavioral Therapy for OCD and Its Subtypes*, 2nd Ed. New York, NY: Guilford Press, p. 336.
   Mataix-Cols, D., Marks, I.M., Greist, J.H., Kobak, K.A., and Baer, L. (2002). Obsessive-compulsive symptom dimensions as predictors of compliance with and response to behavior therapy: Results from a controlled trial. *Psychotherapy and Psychosomatics*, 71, 255-262.

7. Abramowitz, J.S. (2018). *Getting over OCD: A 10-step workbook for taking back your life*, 2nd ed. New York, NY: Guilford Press, p. 100.
8. Abramowitz, J.S. (2018). *Getting over OCD: A 10-step workbook for taking back your life*, 2nd ed. New York, NY: Guilford Press, p. 37.
9. Abramowitz, J.S. (2018). *Getting over OCD: A 10-step workbook for taking back your life*, 2nd ed. New York, NY: Guilford Press, p. 37.
10. Abramowitz, J.S. (2018). *Getting over OCD: A 10-step workbook for taking back your life*, 2nd ed. New York, NY: Guilford Press.
11. Hyman, B.M. and Pedrick, C. (2010). *The OCD Workbook: Your Guide to Breaking Free from Obsessive-Compulsive Disorder*, 3rd Ed. Oakland, CA: New Harbinger Publications.
12. Abramowitz, J.S. (2018). *Getting over OCD: A 10-step workbook for taking back your life*, 2nd ed. New York, NY: Guilford Press, p. 93.
13. Abramowitz, J.S., Deacon, B.J., and Whiteside, S.P.H. (2019). *Exposure Therapy for Anxiety: Principles and Practice*, 2nd ed. New York, NY: Guilford Press, p. 18.
14. Mazza, M.T. (2020). *The ACT Workbook for OCD: Mindfulness, Acceptance & Exposure Skills to Live Well with Obsessive-Compulsive Disorder*. Oakland, CA: New Harbinger Publications, Inc. p. 26.
15. For the most widely used self-help workbook for OCD see: Hyman, B.M. and Pedrick, C. (2010). *The OCD Workbook: Your Guide to Breaking Free from Obsessive-Compulsive Disorder*, 3rd Ed. Oakland, CA: New Harbinger Publications.
    Another excellent workbook for OCD by the leading scholar in field is:
    Abramowitz, J.S. (2018). *Getting over OCD: A 10-step workbook for taking back your life*, 2nd ed. New York, NY: Guilford Press.
16. See https://iocdf.org/about-ocd/ocd-treatment/erp/
17. Abramowitz, J.S. (2018). *Getting over OCD: A 10-step workbook for taking back your life*, 2nd ed. New York, NY: Guilford Press, pp. 131-132.
18. Abramowitz, J.S. (2018). *Getting over OCD: A 10-step workbook for taking back your life*, 2nd ed. New York, NY: Guilford Press, p. 200.
19. Abramowitz, J.S., Deacon, B.J., and Whiteside, S.P.H. (2019). *Exposure Therapy for Anxiety: Principles and Practice*, 2nd ed. New York, NY: Guilford Press, p. 201. (Italics in the original)
20. Abramowitz, J.S. (2018). *Getting over OCD: A 10-step workbook for taking back your life*, 2nd ed. New York, NY: Guilford Press, p. 92.
21. Abramowitz, J.S. (2018). *Getting over OCD: A 10-step workbook for taking back your life*, 2nd ed. New York, NY: Guilford Press, p. 109.
22. Abramowitz, J.S. (2018). *Getting over OCD: A 10-step workbook for taking back your life*, 2nd ed. New York, NY: Guilford Press, p. 171.
23. Abramowitz, J.S. (2018). *Getting over OCD: A 10-step workbook for taking back your life*, 2nd ed. New York, NY: Guilford Press, p. 171.
24. Clark, D.A. (2020). *Cognitive-Behavioral Therapy for OCD and Its Subtypes*, 2nd Ed. New York, NY: Guilford Press, p. 318.
25. Clark, D.A. (2020). *Cognitive-Behavioral Therapy for OCD and Its Subtypes*, 2nd Ed. New York, NY: Guilford Press, p. 318.
26. Abramowitz, J.S. (2018). *Getting over OCD: A 10-step workbook for taking back your life*, 2nd ed. New York, NY: Guilford Press, Step 6 pp. 143-166.

NOTES

9. PHASE III: ACCEPTANCE AND COMMITMENT THERAPY (ACT)

1. * Pronounced like the word *act* as in action, not A.C.T. The theorists of this therapy model want to convey that therapy requires the patient to act according to committed values in response to difficulties or stressors.
2. Abramowitz, J.S. (2018). *Getting over OCD: A 10-step workbook for taking back your life*, 2nd ed. New York, NY: Guilford Press, pp. 1-2.
3. Hayes, Steven C., Strosahl, Kirk D., and Wilson, Kelly G. (2012). *Acceptance and Commitment Therapy: The Process and Practice of Mindful Change (2 ed.)*. New York: Guilford Press. p. 240.
4. See https://millenniumconsulting.co.nz/acceptance-and-commitment-therapy/
5. As cited in: Mazza, M.T. (2020). *The ACT Workbook for OCD: Mindfulness, Acceptance & Exposure Skills to Live Well with Obsessive-Compulsive Disorder*. Oakland, CA: New Harbinger Publications, Inc. p. 150.
6. See http://mindsetfamilytherapy.com/
7. Mazza, M.T. (2020). *The ACT Workbook for OCD: Mindfulness, Acceptance & Exposure Skills to Live Well with Obsessive-Compulsive Disorder*. Oakland, CA: New Harbinger Publications, Inc. p. 172.
8. See https://www.lifechangehypnotherapy.com.au/mindfulness.html
9. Weir, K.N., Greaves, M., Denno, R., Kelm, C., Ragu, R. (2014). Scrupulosity: Practical Treatment Considerations Drawn from Clinical and Ecclesiastical Experiences with Latter-day Saint Persons Struggling with Religiously-oriented Obsessive Compulsive Disorder, *Issues in Religion and Psychotherapy*, Vol. 36, No. 1, pp. 57-69.
10. For a small sampling of the numerous studies Dr. Twohig has completed on ACT and OCD see:

    Twohig, M. P., Abramowitz, J. S., Smith, B. M., Fabricant, L. E., Jacoby, R. J., Morrison, K. L., Bluett, E.J., Reuman, L., Blakey, S.M., & Ledermann, T. (2018). Adding acceptance and commitment therapy to exposure and response prevention for obsessive-compulsive disorder: A randomized controlled trial. Behaviour Research & Therapy, 108, 1–9.

    Twohig, M. P. & Smith B. M. (2015). Targeting the function of inner experiences in obsessive compulsive and related disorders. Current Opinion in Psychology, 2, 32-37.

    Twohig, M. P., Morrison, K. L., & Bluett, E. J. (2014). Acceptance and commitment therapy for OCD and OC-spectrum disorders. Current Psychiatry Reviews, 10, 296-307.

    Twohig, M. P., Whittal, M. L., Cox, J. M., & Gunter, R. (2010). An initial investigation into the processes of change in ACT, CT, and ERP for OCD. International Journal of Behavioral Consultation & Therapy, 6(1), 67–83.
11. Dehlin, J. P, Morrison, K. L., & Twohig, M. P. (2013). Acceptance and commitment therapy as a treatment for scrupulosity in obsessive compulsive disorder. Behavior Modification, 37, 409-430
12. This list and the descriptions of the metaphors are based on descriptions found in the following texts:

Abramowitz, J.S. (2018). *Getting over OCD: A 10-step workbook for taking back your life,* 2nd ed. New York, NY: Guilford Press, p. 182.

Abramowitz, J.S., Deacon, B.J., and Whiteside, S.P.H. (2019). *Exposure Therapy for Anxiety: Principles and Practice,* 2nd ed. New York, NY: Guilford Press, pp. 384-399.

13. Abramowitz, J.S. (2018). *Getting over OCD: A 10-step workbook for taking back your life,* 2nd ed. New York, NY: Guilford Press, p. 123.
14. Abramowitz, J.S. (2018). *Getting over OCD: A 10-step workbook for taking back your life,* 2nd ed. New York, NY: Guilford Press, p. 216.
15. See Andrea Barrocas Gottlieb (2016). DBT 101: What Does Dialectical Even Mean? https://www.sheppardpratt.org/news-views/story/dbt-101-what-does-dialectical-even-mean/

10. WHAT EVERY BISHOP OR PRESIDENT OUGHT TO KNOW ABOUT SCRUPULOSITY: CONSULTING WITH PRIESTHOOD LEADERS

1. * All names and other identifying information about individuals used as examples in this book have been changed to protect their confidentiality.
2. Ciarrocchi, J. W. (1995). *The Doubting Disease: Help for Scrupulosity and Religious Compulsions.* Mahwah, NJ: Paulist Press.
3. Santa, T.M. (2017). *Understanding scrupulosity: Questions and encouragement,* 3rd ed. Liguori, MO: Liguori Publications.
4. For the original version by Father Santa see: https://scrupulousanonymous.org/wp-content/uploads/2015/10/Ten_Commandments_for_the_Scrupulous_2013.pdf
5. Glenn L. Pace, (2005). "Confidence and Self-Worth." *Ensign,* January 2005. https://www.Churchofjesuschrist.org/study/ensign/2005/01/confidence-and-self-worth?lang=eng
6. Glenn L. Pace, (2005). "Confidence and Self-Worth." *Ensign,* January 2005. https://www.Churchofjesuschrist.org/study/ensign/2005/01/confidence-and-self-worth?lang=eng
7. Abramowitz, J.S. (2018). *Getting over OCD: A 10-step workbook for taking back your life,* 2nd ed. New York, NY: Guilford Press, p. 16.
8. * Remember Dr. Joseph Ciarrochi's definition of scrupulosity in his book *The Doubting Disease* – "seeing sin where there is none." Competent therapists will often use the patient's concerns about things they think may or might be a sin (but are not actual sins) as a means of accomplishing ERP work.
9. Tad R. Callister, (2019). *A Case for the Book of Mormon.* Salt Lake City, UT: Deseret Book Company, p. 168.
10. Richard G. Scott - Peace of Conscience and Peace of Mind (Oct. 2004 General Conference), https://www.lds.org/general-conference/2004/10/peace-of-conscience-and-peace-of-mind?lang=eng

Made in the USA
Middletown, DE
03 May 2022